This richly Reformed, experiential treatise opens up the great blessings of looking in faith to the person of Jesus Christ. Bonar shows us that from the new birth to one's passage through death into glory, Christ is everything to the believer. In fact, He Himself, as revealed in His Word and promises, is the essence of our assurance of faith. This book is a great help to any true Christian who longs to grow in the Christian life in full-orbed assurance.

Joel R. Beeke
President, Puritan Reformed Theological Seminary
Grand Rapids, Michigan

This little book reminds us that salvation is not found in bare belief but enfleshed Deity. Our salvation is a person – the Lord Jesus Christ. Bonar's short chapters stir our affections as we ponder the Lord's personal beauty and sufficiency. In this book you will behold the glorious King in a fresh way, and gain new muscle as you cling to the Christ-Ark.

Natalie Brand
Bible Teacher and Author of
Priscilla, Where Are You? A Call to Joyful Theology

The brevity of this book is no indicator of the immense help it can provide for any who desire to grow in knowing Jesus. With each page, Bonar carefully and consistently lifts up the person of Christ and exhorts us with reasons to keep our eyes fixed on him. My heart was stirred with fresh affection for my Savior, and I pray yours would be as well.

Matt Boswell
Pastor, The Trails Church
Hymnwriter; Assistant Professor of Church Music and
Worship, The Southern Baptist Theological Seminary

The Person
of Christ

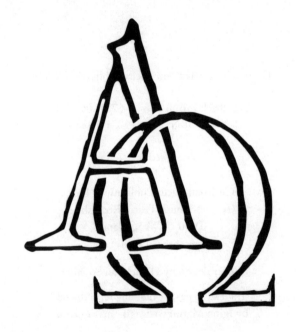

Finding Assurance by Walking With Jesus

Andrew Bonar

CHRISTIAN
HERITAGE

Scripture quotations are based on the *King James Version*.

Hardback ISBN: 978–1–5271–0971–1
E-book ISBN: 978-1-5271-1023-6

Published in 2023
by
Christian Focus Publications Ltd,
Geanies House, Fearn, Ross–shire
IV20 1TW, Scotland
www.christianfocus.com

Cover design by Daniel Van Straaten

The Fell Types are digitally reproduced
by Igino Marini www.iginomarini.com

Printed and bound by Gutenberg, Malta

CONTENTS

FOREWORD

In this new edition, no change of any importance has been made beyond the correction of errata, and extending the texts quoted. The object of the book is to draw more attention to the great subject of connecting at all times the Person of Christ with His work. This is a point which the experience of the most solid believers has testified to as of vast importance. Toplady quotes the following case from the diary of one who afterwards preached Christ, Mr Thomas Cole. Listen to his interesting statement:

> I was convinced I could be saved no other way than by grace, if I could but find grace enough. But at that time I saw more in my own sin than in God's mercy. But this put me on a further inquiry after the grace of God, because my life lay upon it: and then I was brought to the Gospel. When, however, I came to the Gospel, I met with the law in it; that is, I was for turning the Gospel into law. I began to settle myself upon Gospel-duties, such as repentance,

humiliation, believing, praying; and (I know not how) I forgot the promise of grace which first brought me to the Gospel. Soon, I found I could neither believe nor pray as the Gospel required. While I was in this plunge, it pleased the Lord to direct me to study the Person of Christ, whom I looked on as the great undertaker in the work of man's salvation! And truly here I may say, as Paul did, 'It pleased God to reveal His Son in me.' God overcame my heart with this. I saw so much mercy in His mercy, so much love in His love, so much grace in His grace, that I knew not what to liken it to. And here my heart broke, I knew not how! Before this faith came, I knew not how to secure myself against past, present, and future sins: but there was that largeness of grace, that all-sufficiency of mercy, that infinity of righteousness, discovered to me in Christ, that I found sufficient for all the days of my life.

GLASGOW, June, 1858.

I

STATEMENT OF THE FACT THAT THE PERSON OF CHRIST IS THE ESSENCE OF THE GLAD TIDINGS

From the beginning, the Gospel has come to the awakened sinner with the same consciousness of important news to tell, as that messenger who ran to David, after the battle of Mahanaim, exclaiming 'All is well!' But even as the burden of that message brought by Ahimaaz was simply victory, without any narrative of details, so was the Old Testament proclamation of the good news to our earth. There was still need of a Cushi to give details; and Cushi did come upon the heels of Ahimaaz, telling that the essence of the victory lay in the fact of the leader of the host being himself slain. It is thus the New Testament has overtaken the Old, proclaiming, 'Tidings, O earth! Tidings! It is the Son of God who has died, satisfying the Law of His Father, and establishing His throne.'

In the synagogue of Pisidian Antioch (Acts 13:32) Paul announced to the intently listening audience, 'We declare unto you glad tidings!' and forthwith added that the promise made to the fathers was now fulfilled in Jesus risen. It was as if he had said, 'The voice from the excellent glory cries, Hear the beloved Son! and speaks of nothing but what He is, has, and has done.' That vessel which has endured all the storms of wrath, that ark which has borne unmoved the shock of cataracts from the opened windows of heaven, and depths breaking up below, contains everything fitted to meet the sinner's need; and in proportion as the Holy Ghost reveals this Person to the awakened sinner, there will come to light a store of all things suited to the cravings of an immortal soul.

When the sinner has got any clear discovery of this glorious Person, he is a saved man; for so we find written in Galatians 1:13-16, 'Ye have heard of my conversation in time past ... But it pleased God ... to reveal his Son in me.' Matthew 16:16-17, 'Simon Peter answered and said, Thou art the Christ, the Son of the living God. And Jesus answered and said unto him, Blessed art thou, Simon Barjona; for flesh and blood hath not revealed it unto thee, but my Father which is in heaven.'

Resting on this Person for salvation is called 'Faith in Jesus Christ'. In this faith, there is an intellectual act – namely, the apprehending of the meaning of what is stated concerning Jesus. But this apprehension of the meaning of what is stated, or testified, concerning Jesus, is but the avenue that leads on to the magnificent mansion. It leads the soul to the Person of whom these things are declared. It never is the belief of bare propositions that saves the soul; for these have to do only with the understanding. Propositions, however weighty, must guide us onward to the Person who is the essence of the testimony; they are made use of for this end by the same Holy Spirit who enlightens our once carnal understanding to see the real truth.[1]

The belief of the testimony, or record, concerning the Son of God, our Saviour, is the porch of the building, through which we pass into the audience–chamber and meet the Living Inhabitant, full of light, and life, and love.

There is a twofold remedy required to meet the exigencies of a fallen soul.

1. The soul must feel entirely delivered from that guilt which has compelled the Holy God to withdraw. The sinner's soul is by nature laden with guilt, the guilt of original and actual sin; and until this guilt is altogether taken away, there can be no freedom of access to God. But remove this barrier, and then the Holy God may meet the sinner, and the sinner may run to the open arms of the Holy God. This is the bringing of the conscience to solid rest.

2. The soul has feelings, emotions, affections, which constitute what we call in common language the heart of the man. The heart, then, must be brought to its rest, as

---

1. 'Though faith be radically in the understanding, yet it operates on the will which embraces the object' (FISHER'S Catechism). 'Faith is begun in the head, but not perfected till it comes into the heart' (ROGERS of Dedham). 'Faith is not so much a disposition of the mind toward the truth, as a disposition of the heart toward Christ, produced by means of the truth' (SIEVEWRIGHT). 'The soul in believing closes with the Person of Christ. He is the principal object, though not the immediate object of faith' (FRASER of Brae).

well as the conscience; and it will be brought to rest, if you can find for it an object vast enough, rich enough, and so accommodated to its frame as to give ample scope for the exercise of all its powers, and the play of all its feelings.

Now, both these ends are answered when the soul discovers the Person of the God–man. There it is that the twofold remedy is found. For now, the conscience, enabled by the Holy Spirit to discern and examine the treasures stored up in the God–man Mediator, finds all the materials needful to its pacification and rest, inasmuch as His obedience to the law and the satisfaction rendered by Him for dishonour done to it, are efficacious beyond measure. And next, when enabled by the same Spirit of truth to explore the wealth of sympathy, and tenderness, and brotherly feeling, wherewith the God–man is fraught, and which is given forth from the side of His humanity, the man finds therein such an object as his heart craved, an object on which his heart can repose.

It is now that he tastes 'The Bread of Life.' It is only now that he knows the meaning of making the Saviour his meat and drink (John 6:52); for it is now that he has found out the entire remedy for his case in the person of a Mediator, who unites the human nature with the Divine, and uses both in dealing with man. Finding flesh and blood (and, of course, all that is peculiar to a frame wherein flesh and blood are ingredients) in a Saviour, whose doing, dying, and rising again brought in everlasting righteousness, the man can say – 'Every part of my nature has been thought upon, and provision has been made for all my feelings and faculties, as well as conscience: this is indeed meat and drink to me! His flesh is meat indeed! His blood is drink indeed!'

Our purpose, then, is to enter into details whereby we may show that the Person of Christ is, and has always been, the essence of the Gospel. The glad tidings of great joy all cluster round that Person; invitations and calls draw us to Him; and warrants for believing the Gospel are in reality testimonies, the drift of which is mainly this – to fix our eye upon that Person's self, and assure us of the capabilities of His heart and arm.

And no wonder that it should be so; for He is GOD manifest in the flesh. To see Him is to see GOD in the attitude of redemption. To see Him is to see the GOD of holy love putting Himself in a position wherein He might be able, justly and honourably, to save sinners. To see Him is to see Godhead finding a way of coming to sinners with open arms, and yet remaining as holy, and just, and true, as from all eternity.

To show that this is the essence of the Gospel may be important alike to saints who already fear the Lord, and to sinners who are only groping for Him. Both are thus led directly to confront God, – 'God manifest in the flesh,' in 'whom are hid all the treasures of wisdom and knowledge.' The saint finds that here he floats upon an ocean of grace, and that the more constantly he abides here, the more is he blessed. The seeking sinner finds that his perplexities are cleared away, when he is dealing, not with abstract truth, nor with cold statements, but with a Person, and that person full of grace and truth.

'Come, now' (come, I pray you; come, I beseech you), 'let us reason together, saith the LORD' (Isa. 1:18). Here are two parties before us – not one party dealing with the words and declarations of another, but two parties confronting each other. It is a meeting of spirit with spirit – the spirit of man with God who is spirit. It is the living man coming to hear the living God tell His heart and ways.

Bunyan, in his *Pilgrim's Progress*, represents Christian, when relieved of his burden at the cross, singing with joy –

> Blest cross! blest sepulchre! blest rather be
> THE MAN that there was put to shame for me.

And in his 'Instruction for the Ignorant,' the following dialogue occurs :

> Question. If such a poor sinner as I am would be saved from the wrath to come, how must I believe?
>
> Answer. Thy first question should be, on whom must I believe? John 9:35-36, 'Dost thou believe on the Son of God?' 'Who is He, Lord, that I might believe on Him?'
>
> Q. On whom, then, must I believe?
>
> A. On the Lord Jesus Christ.
>
> Q. Who is Jesus Christ, that I might believe on Him?

A. He is the only-begotten Son of God.

Q. Why must I believe on Him?

A. Because He is the Saviour of the world.

Q. How is He the Saviour of the world?

A. By the Father's designation and sending; for God sent not His Son into the world to condemn the world, but that the world through Him might be saved.

Q. How did He come into the world?

A. In man's flesh – in which flesh He fulfilled the law, died for our sins, conquered the devil and death, and obtained eternal redemption for us.

Q. But is there no other way to be saved but by believing in Jesus Christ?

A. There is no other name given under heaven, among men, whereby we must be saved. And therefore he that believeth not shall be damned. Acts 4:12, 'Neither is there salvation in any other: for there is none other name under heaven given among men, whereby we must be saved.' Mark 16:16, 'But he that believeth not shall be damned.' John 3:18, 36, 'He that believeth on him is not condemned; but he that believeth not is condemned already, because he hath not believed in the name of the only-begotten Son of God.' 'He that believeth on the Son hath everlasting life: and he that believeth not the Son shall not see life; but the wrath of God abideth on him.'

Q. What is believing on Jesus Christ?

A. It is the receiving of Him, with what is in Him, as the gift of God to thee, a sinner. John 1:12, 'To as many as receive him, even to them that believe on his name, he gave power to become sons of God.'

Q. What is in Jesus Christ to encourage me to receive Him?

A. Infinite righteousness to justify thee, and the Spirit without measure to sanctify thee.

Q. Is this made mine if I receive Christ?

A. Yes, if you receive Him as God offereth Him to thee.

Q. How doth God offer Him to me?

A. Even as a rich man freely offereth an alms to a beggar – and so must thou receive Him. John 6:32, 33, 34, 35, 'My Father giveth you the true bread from heaven; for the bread of God is he that cometh down from heaven, and giveth life unto the world.' Then said they unto Him, 'Lord, evermore give us this bread.' And Jesus said unto them, 'I am the bread of life: he that cometh to me shall never hunger, and he that believeth on me shall never thirst.'

THE GOSPEL, FROM THE FALL TO THE DAY OF THE APOSTLES, WAS FOUND IN THE PERSON OF THE SAVIOUR

In the New Testament, the name of 'Mystery' is often attached to the truths that form the Gospel. The chief part of this mystery, or 'truth hidden from eternity in God' (Eph. 3:9), concerned the Person of the Saviour. When the real nature of this person was unfolded, other things, which had been dark, began forthwith to emerge from their obscurity and appear distinct. It could not but be plain now why blood should be the means of atonement, since the blood is the out-poured life, and the out-poured life is the life of Him who is the Son of God. The blood poured out in every sacrifice spoke of some one giving his life; but the nature of the effect of this blood-shedding could be understood only when the person, in his worth and dignity, became known.

Hence it was that all patriarchs and ancient saints were directed unceasingly to the Living One as the well-spring of their bliss. Their hands were every day fully employed in offering sacrifice, but yet, all the while, their eye was looking beyond that sacrifice for some one yet to come, who was to cast light on this service and make them 'perfect as pertaining to the conscience' (Heb. 9:9). Their thoughts (however confusedly) passed from the types of the work of Christ on to the expected Person of Christ. And hence Paul declares, the discovery of who this coming one was, to be the 'making manifest of the mystery.' When writing to the Romans (16:25-26), he thus speaks, 'According to my gospel, and the preaching of (i.e., proclamation concerning) the Lord Jesus Christ; according to the revelation of the mystery, which had been kept secret since the world began, but now is made manifest.'

It seems that ancient saints were aware that the Person of the Coming One was to cast light on all the ceremonials and ordinances which they were taught to observe. For Peter, in telling of 'salvation,' states that the prophets who inquired and searched diligently into it, bent their chief attention toward 'the sufferings of Christ and the glory that should follow' (1 Pet. 1:10-11). And the same is implied by the words of our Lord to His disciples in reference to His being now at length among them in the flesh, when, turning to them, He said, 'Blessed are the eyes that see the things which ye see; for I tell you that many prophets and kings have desired to see those things which ye see, and have not seen them, and to hear those things which ye hear, and have not heard them' (Luke 10:23-24).

Onward from the hour when first the announcement of a Saviour was made in the words, 'The seed of the Woman shall bruise the head of the serpent,' the anxious inquiries of all saints were directed toward this person, to know who and what He was to be. The case of the Old Testament believers was like that of exiles, who had got the promise of return from banishment, but who saw not the means by which they were to be transported homeward from their dreary island of captivity. At length, one whose eye has looked through the telescope comes among them, points them to a speck in the distant horizon, telling them that yonder is the vessel sent to carry them home. They have had intimations of their sovereign's pardon and goodwill already, but this is the most satisfactory proof of it. Accordingly, hour after hour do they keep their eye fixed on that distant object, and their joy rises in proportion as they are able distinctly to discern that yonder speck is indeed a vessel, bearing colours that proclaim from what land it has come. Having in their possession letters sealed with the king's seal, which speak of actual deliverance to be brought them when such a vessel should touch their coasts, they reckon its arrival to be their grand hope, and expect to find therein everything needed for their immediate recall. This was the position of Old Testament saints: they were gazing on this speck in the distant ocean. The vessel was seen by Job a little more distinctly than by previous patriarchs, when he sang, 'I know that my Redeemer liveth, and that He will stand on the earth at the latter day' and yet more plainly by those who heard that He was to be 'Abraham's seed,' and 'Shiloh' from the tribe of Judah, and 'David's son,' as well as 'David's Lord.'

A still clearer sight was gained when Isaiah stood and cried, 'To us a child is born, to us a son is given, and his name shall be called Wonderful, Counsellor, the Mighty God!' (Isa. 9:6). And yet more, when Zechariah declared that he heard the Almighty call Him 'The Man that is my Fellow!' (Zech. 13:7). The vessel was now seen with joyful distinctness, and the hope of the Lord's banished ones grew brighter and brighter, as Malachi (3:1) cried, 'The LORD whom ye seek shall suddenly come to his temple.'

In revealing salvation to men, in early ages, the Lord arranged His discoveries in such a way as necessarily led them to give the Person of the Redeemer a prominent place in all their thoughts. It was with them more the Redeemer than even redemption. They did not well know how this Noah was to save them, or how he was to guide the ark through floods, rushing from below and from above; and how, over these strange billows, he was finally to land it in the strange harbour of Ararat. But what of this, if they were really trusting themselves to this Noah, and were identified with him in his undertaking? He knew, and he would accomplish all.

It was thus also, in great measure, with the disciples and followers of our Lord in the days of His flesh. They knew amazingly little of His work in its details, but truly they clung to His Person. Is there any hint of their loving any other as they loved Him? They rested on the Shepherd's shoulder, and in so doing were safe. They did not know how this Shepherd was to save them; how He was to deliver them from the lion and the bear, and carry them over the burning desert of wrath; but still, they were safe, because they rested on Him. They clung to the right person, and committed themselves to His wisdom, and power, and love.

Was this not the essence of old Simeon's hope of salvation? Was he not the traveller arrived at the sources of the Nile, surveying the fountain from which living waters had flowed, and were yet to flow, to fertilise the earth? When he took up the child Jesus in his arms, the aged saint exclaimed, 'Now thou art letting thy servant depart in peace, according to thy word, for mine eyes have seen thy salvation' (Luke 2:29-30).

What else but a message about His Person was the gospel preached by the Angel at Bethlehem, which sent home the shepherds 'glorifying and praising God'? The words were, 'A Saviour is born, which is Christ the Lord' (Luke 2:11). This is what the Angel calls 'good tidings of great joy.' Let wise men and shepherds, let Mary and Joseph, let Zechariah and Elizabeth, let Anna and Simeon, let all who hear this proclaimed, cling to this Person, and in Him they shall find salvation. They may not see in what manner, or by what process, He is to save them, but cling to this Person, and all shall be well.

The Baptist comes forth. His preaching is a constant pointing to 'the Lamb of God.' His finger is ever directing men to Him. All good news is yonder, and bliss is in that Person, 'the Son of God,' who stands among you. He saw the Spirit descend on Him, and ever after bare record that 'He was THE SON OF GOD' (John 1:34).

'Herein is great joy for all people! The Person we cling to for salvation turns out to be "SON OF GOD!" The promised Seed of Abraham, and the Seed of the Woman, in whom all our hope is treasured up, is none other than the SON OF GOD! What may we now expect of Him! How full may our cup now be!' Some such must have been the feelings of those who first saw the glorious truth, especially when the discovery burst fresh upon them. The news would fly from one to another – 'The Messiah is none other than God! GOD is manifest in flesh'[1] (1 Tim. 3:16).

And little as they knew of the mode of His working, or how He was to proceed in going forward to save them, they clung to His Person closer than ever. As their fathers followed the cloudy pillar, longing to see the face of Him who sat therein, so they followed Jesus, longing to see what He would yet reveal of Himself and of His ways.

And they were right in so clinging to Him. Peter was asked, along with his fellow–disciples, 'Whom do men say that I the Son of man am?' (Matt. 16:13), obviously with the view of bringing out fully who this Saviour was who appeared under that form. And his reply, 'Thou art Christ, the Son of the living God,' (Matt. 16:16) drew forth the declaration, 'Blessed art thou, Simon Barjona! Flesh and

---

1. Even as saints still feel, when the Holy Ghost sets it very vividly before them. Howell Harris, in one of his letters, saith: 'O the mystery! That this man is God! He wept. He travelled, bore cold, rain, hunger, and thirst; all reproach, shame, and all other sorrows for me. My loving, everlasting brother! Sure this Lord is my love! My soul within me is lost in wonder, and melts like wax. O this love! This mysterious, unfathomable love!'

blood hath not revealed it unto thee, but my Father which is in heaven' (Matt. 16:17). So great was the discovery – He that is come to save is God! For such a one must be able to save. He cannot but bring full salvation – a salvation that will have length and breadth in it, height and depth, sufficient every way for a sinner.

It was thus also that Peter made a similar confession on another occasion (John 6:69) with great emphasis: 'We believe and are sure that thou art the Christ, the Son of the living God.' He adheres to this Person; and yet so little does he understand the work which that Person is to perform, that on the mention of suffering, and reproach, and death (Matt. 16:21), 'that he must suffer many things of the elders, and chief priests, and scribes, and be killed,' though followed by resurrection, he peremptorily insists that the idea was utterly inconsistent with his Lord's dignity and character. We are ready to think that ignorance of, or mistake regarding, the work of Christ is as hurtful and dangerous as misunderstanding His Person. But the Lord Himself lays somewhat greater stress upon our not mistaking His Person. That Person is the mine; His work is one of the treasures which come to the surface when the mine is wrought.

It was not enough that a Jew confessed Jesus to be the Christ – the Messiah. He might do this and yet be ignorant of the Saviour. He must know the Messiah to be the SON OF GOD, if he was to know true salvation. For what could the Messiah do for sinners if (like the Christ of Socinians) He were only a superior, though extraordinary man – and what could the Messiah do for such sinners as we are, if He were (like the Christ of Arians) only at the top of the angelic scale? We needed a Messiah who could 'save to the uttermost,' and none other than the SON OF GOD could stretch the cords of salvation thus far. It is on this account that our Lord Himself says most solemnly in John 8:24, 'If ye believe not that I am he, ye shall die in your sins.' He had declared Himself 'from above' (v. 23), and 'not of this world,' and had said, 'I am not alone, but I and the Father that sent me' (v. 16). And now, turning to the cavilling crowd of Pharisees, He looked them in the face, and with awful seriousness and majesty in His tone, assured them, 'If ye believe not I am He (the Person whom I have said I am), ye shall die in your sins.'

But did not the disciples falter oftentimes in their views of His Person? And did not the ancient saints fall short of knowing the Promised Seed to be GOD THE SON? So far this is true. But at least they expected a Saviour from the Lord Jehovah, and were ready to welcome this Person without faltering or hesitation. Perhaps there were none of those saints who had not some idea, however dim, of God being somehow in the salvation promised; and never certainly did any saved man, in any age, deny or slight the Godhead of the Saviour, when revealed to his astonished gaze. Every saved soul has been too glad to find God Himself the Saviour; 'Behold God is my salvation,' – and seeing Him has said, 'I will trust and not be afraid; for the LORD JEHOVAH is my strength and my song; he also is become my salvation. Therefore with joy shall ye draw water out of the wells of salvation' (Isa. 12:2-3).

> Hidden from all ages past
> Was the Cross's mystery;
> Death a while a veil had cast
> O'er that first dear family;
> But they saw Him and believed,
> And as Lord and God received.

The saints' hopes have, in every age, revolved around 'Him that cometh in the name of the Lord.' To have the heart fixed on the Lord, and on Him whom He was to send, is the heart and kernel of ancient faith. It is the Old Testament form of our Gospel that we hear when, in the 'song of songs,' the Spouse dwells upon the Beloved, and repeats and reiterates His praises. Who this Beloved is seems scarcely known; He has a veil on His Person; but, nevertheless, there is a mysterious strength of feeling between this Beloved and those who sing of Him, arising from the secret fact that GOD THE SON is the Beloved under the veil.

'Who is this that cometh up from the wilderness, leaning upon her beloved?' (Song 8:5). This surely is a sketch of Patriarchal and Jewish faith – just as the figure of the 'Sheep on the Shepherd's shoulder,' so often appearing on the tombs in the catacombs at Rome, is the symbol of the same faith in New Testament times.

When the Apostle John, in his first Epistle, thus writes (1 John 5:20) to the saints: 'And we know that the SON

OF GOD is come!' he unquestionably is uttering, and intending to utter, the full gospel–privileges of believers. He says that this distinguished them from the world – viz., they know that the promised Seed had come, and that He was the Son of God. By that time the Church had arrived at clearer light; for John in his gospel (6:69) tells of Peter's glowing animation as he confessed, Thou art Messiah, the Son of the living God; and of Martha's unhesitating declaration, that, as a matter of course, she, a disciple of the Lord Jesus, believed that He was 'The Messiah, the Son of God, who should come into the world.' Nor was it otherwise when disciples were able to give more precise details of the Person, as we see in the Ethiopian eunuch's joyful confession, 'I believe that Jesus Christ is the Son of God!' We may conceive his feelings – he had journeyed far, many a hundred miles – risking the favour of his queen, and caring little for his place of rank. He had sought rest for his awakened soul in vain, even in Jerusalem at their solemn feasts. But a stranger, a true evangelist, is sent to him, as his chariot rolls lazily and silently over the sandy desert–road towards Gaza, and finds him reading in the fifty–third of Isaiah concerning one 'led as a Lamb to the slaughter.' The stranger tells him who this was, and how, and why, and when He had been led to death; and proclaims the tidings, that 'this Lamb was Son of God!' What a flash of amazement and delight passes over the Ethiopian's countenance! He is under the teaching of the Holy Ghost (for it was He who was hovering over him, vv. 29-39), and saw in a moment what that fact implied.

Here is room for my soul now! Here my burdened spirit may repose.[2]

The Person who is the Lamb is Son of God! Here is not a narrow point of a rock, rising above the surrounding water, but no more than barely sufficient for one to stand upon: here is a broad continent to which the eye sees no limit! With what exultation is he filled in confessing, 'I believe that Jesus Christ is the Son of God!'

We are wrong, in our day, when we speak more of the work of Christ than of His Person – directing more attention to the shadow afforded by the great Rock than to the Rock itself. This is not done in the Apostolic Epistles – there, the work is not separated from the worker, but ever kept beside him, and He beside the work.[3]

In Romans 3:22, the righteousness is said to be, not 'by faith in the work' of Christ, but 'by faith of Jesus Christ, unto all and upon all them that believe.' And again in verses 24 and 25, 'Justified freely by His grace, through the redemption that is in Christ Jesus, whom God has set forth to be a propitiation through faith in his blood.'

---

2. 'If you ask why I believe on the Son of God – if you intend what is the formal reason, ground, and warranty, whereon I thus believe in Him, or place my confidence in Him – I say it is only this, that "He is over all, God blessed for ever". And were He not so, I could not believe in Him. The divine nature is the reason of it, but His divine Person is the object of it' (OWEN).

3. As Augustine (Confessions, Book 5.1) says of the other works of God, 'The soul bending over the things thou hast made, and passing on to Thee who hast made them, there finds its refreshment and true strength.'

Again, in chapter 5:1-2, 'We have peace through our Lord Jesus Christ by whom also we have access by faith into this grace wherein we stand.' Again, in chapter 6:4, 'We are buried with him,' or, verse 8, 'we are dead with him.'

Union to Him, as our representative, is the very heart of the argument. Or, if the apostle is writing freely about Christian blessings, as in Ephesians chapter 1, we are told of being 'blessed with all spiritual blessings, in heavenly places, in Christ' and (vv. 6-7) of being 'accepted in the beloved, in whom we have redemption.'

These men of God, whom the Holy Spirit inspired, lead the sinner to the shade of the Plant of Renown; but all the while they are occupying his attention by pointing out the Plant itself – its majestic form, and glorious growth, and ever green foliage, and the immense sweep of its branches; and while they are thus engaged, the traveller is refreshed tenfold more effectually than if he had been content merely to stretch himself along in motionless repose beneath the spreading boughs. 'We have boldness to enter the holiest by the blood of Jesus,' says the apostle; but forthwith he adds, 'Having an high priest over the House of God' (Heb. 10:19, 21).

The Lord's Supper also, if it be rightly understood, cannot fail to fix our eye on the Person. No doubt it speaks of the death, and of the New Covenant ratified by that death, and so of pardon and holiness, and all other connected benefits. But who can overlook the Benefactor amid His benefits? Are we not led directly, at that holy ordinance, to His Person, inasmuch as union to Him is the truth most remarkably exhibited therein? Union to Him who gives us His blood to ratify the New Covenant, and who gives us Himself as the food of our souls, is surely the very essence of the Lord's Supper. We show His 'death,' with our eye on 'Him who died.' We show His sufferings of body and of soul, with our eye on the suffering one. We think of our sins requiring such a remedy – our wounds needing such balm – but still with our eye fixed on the Person whose stripes heal us. 'Till He come' fixes yet again our eye on Himself, so that its gaze passes from the day of His agony onward to the day of His glory, and looks out for the 'King in His beauty,' as well as looks back on His marred form.

The Holy Ghost delights in the Person of Christ. It was to honour not only His work, but Himself, that He descended on the day of His baptism. It is not merely the work, but the doer of it, that He delights to honour. The expressions, 'He shall glorify me' (John 16:14), and 'He shall testify of me' (John 15:26), do not, of course, exclude His work; they necessarily imply it; only they do not mean His work apart from Himself. The Holy Ghost will ever honour the setting forth of the Person who has given glory to God in the highest, and is Himself God over all. We may expect Him to bless us most when we are rather dwelling on the benefits as so many proofs of the Benefactor's heart, than stopping short at these benefits, seeking no more than how to make them our own. The hospital, with its ample accommodation, and its stores of medicine and nourishment, and its supply of all that the sick, however many, can require, with access free to all, at every hour of night or day, this is one thing – but how much better, when besides, we have the presence of the founder and Physician Himself, passing through every room – bending over every sick–bed – uttering words and beaming forth looks of sympathy. Would you commend the place, and forget the physician? And will the Holy Ghost commend the Saviour's benefits, if thereby you are to be led to overlook Him?

3

THE HELP AFFORDED BY CHRIST'S PERSON TO A SOUL SEEKING TO KNOW SIN AND THE APPLICATION OF SALVATION

Many of the early fathers use the word 'theology,' in the sense of 'A discoursing upon the Divinity of Christ,' and they called the Apostle John 'the Divine,' or 'the Theologue,' because he speaks so fully of the Word made flesh. To these Fathers all knowledge of God seemed comprehended in knowing Him who reveals the Father. And following their principles, we maintain that all real knowledge of God's salvation is to be attained by becoming acquainted with Him who is the Saviour sent of God.

In the days of the Reformation, we find Fox, the martyrologist, telling Roman Catholics that, 'as there is no gift of God given to man, no virtue, work, merit, nor anything else, that is part or cause of salvation, but only this gift of faith to believe in Christ Jesus' – so also 'neither does faith, as it is only a bare quality or action in man's mind, itself justify, unless it be directed to the body of

Christ crucified as its object, of whom it receiveth all its virtue.'[1]

In all ages of the Church, to know 'Whom we have believed' has been felt to be all–important. In whatever light we view the matter, its importance will appear.

1. It helps us to discover the malignity of sin

Right views of sin have a tendency to lead us to right views of the Person of the Saviour. But the converse also is true; right views of the Saviour's Person lead to right views of sin.

Socinians and Arians have shallow views of sin. They do not see that it deserves never–ending woe and infinite fierceness of wrath; nor do they feel their conscience alarmed at the enormous depravity of nature, and at the fearfully aggravated sins against God which they daily commit. Hence they see not the need they have of a Divine Saviour – one able to bear infinite wrath for the innumerable sins of a multitude whom no man can number.[2]

---

1. Oliver Cromwell, in his day, writes to General Fleetwood: 'Faith as an act yields not perfect peace, but only carries us to Him who is our perfect rest and peace.'

2. The Elect – those given to Christ by His Father from eternity – His sheep – are not few in number, but 'many.' God, out of His mere good pleasure, looking on a world where all alike were already ruined, elected 'many' to everlasting life. Isaiah 53:12, 'He bare the sin of many.' Matthew 20:28, 'Ransom for many'; Matthew 26:28, 'My blood shed for many.' Romans 5:19, 'Many shall be made righteous.' Electing love has laid hold of an innumerable multitude, and drawn them out of the many waters, putting every sin of every one of them on the Almighty's Fellow, the man Christ Jesus, and imparting to them the grace given them in Him before the world began (1 Tim. 1:9.)

They are conscious that if it required the personal interposition of a divine surety to remove it, the sin must be very great; that it must indeed be branded as hateful beyond conception, if, ere it be forgiven, the lawgiver himself must die. From these men, therefore, we learn to judge thus – that if we would feel the enormity of sin aright, we must see it calling for no less a satisfaction than what could be given by God Incarnate.

The Roman Catholic, whose eye turns oftener far to the Virgin Mary than to Mary's Son, has not surely felt the true nature of sin, the rigour of the law, or the terror of divine judgment. Hence, such men are content to seek pardon through a creature's merits, and think that the intercession of a multitude of such creatures may prevail for them. But did they see sin under the teaching of the Spirit, they would trust their pardon to no one but the God–man, Christ Jesus. And, in point of fact, when Romanists are awakened by the Holy Spirit to deep sense of sin, they forthwith begin to feel how insufficient, how unsatisfactory, how incomplete is any kind of peace that does not come from the Incarnate Son of God. They begin to see sin to be such an evil as only God can remedy. From these, therefore, let us learn to judge thus – it is in Christ, the Son of God, substituted for the sinner, that we see the abyss of evil in our sin, and that we become aware that sin is so clamorous for wrath as to be silenced only by the interposed Person of the Son of God.

But turn aside again: approach an infant newly born, drawing its first breath in this fallen world. There is sin in that soul, and small as the sin may seem when compared with that of sinners who have lived forty or seventy years, yet even the sin of that infant is such an evil as nothing can remedy but the blood of the Son of God. If the sin of that infant is to be forgiven, the Son of God must 'pour out His soul unto death' in its behalf.

Set before you any one of your own acts of disobedience, selecting those which may, in your judgment, appear the smallest and slightest. Yet that act was sin – such an act that, ere it can be forgiven and you received into favour, Godhead must be moved! God the Son must rise from His place on the Father's bosom and haste to your rescue. Less than this would be insufficient; less than this would be entirely useless. For the abyss is bottomless. No angel's strength could bear the burden of the wrath due to your one sin, while certainly no angel's love could endure the trial of interposing as your substitute. Sin is something that only God can deal with – a mysteriously tremendous evil.

These lessons are taught us when we fix our attention not on the mere blessing of forgiveness, but also on the Person who brings it. If we were to adopt another plan too commonly pursued, and merely speak of salvation as a work done and finished well – or as a door opened at which the vilest may come in – or as a free invitation to the chief of sinners – we might in that case miss altogether the clear light cast on sin by the Gospel. But on the other hand, connect all with the Person (and in this case with the divine nature of the Person) – show that here is the work of God in our nature, God occupying our law-room – that here is the door of access opened, but only in consequence of Almighty love shedding the blood of the Beloved Son, heaven's Isaac – that here is a free invitation to the vilest, but that it is thus free only because the Saviour who came was Creator of all creatures, and therefore able to fulfil all conditions, and pay the last mite – show all this, and forthwith the light of the cross is cast on sin, and you see it to be an infinite evil, an evil understood by God alone.[3]

Such is the heat of wrath against sin, that unless the 'shadow' which interposed between me and that heat had been the broad, far-extending shadow of a 'Great Rock,' the air around me would have burnt as an oven still. Such is the burden of sin on my single person, that never could I have been lifted up as a 'lively stone,' and my weight borne by the foundation-stone, unless the foundation had been God the Son. Surely, then, it was a gaping wound that sin had made, when such balm alone could heal it. O my soul, thou wert sinking fast in the swelling stream, and none could beat back the might of the wave but God, God in thy nature. A whole Christ was needed by thee, and that Christ, God! – 'I believe that Jesus Christ is the Son of God' (Acts 8:37).

---

3. 'Who can set forth the riches of His death, and the unfathomable abyss of His sufferings? The inexpressible evil of sin appears here more clearly than if we saw all the misery of the damned' (HOWELL HARRIS, Lett. 43).

2. The application of salvation

A sinner may see that there is none other to whom we can go but Jesus only, and yet he may not go. He may imagine difficulties, and magnify these into impossibilities. But it is remarkable how many of these difficulties and apparent impossibilities flow down at the presence of the Person of the Lord – the soul beholding a full Saviour in Him who is God and man in one person. Clement of Rome ('whose name is in the Book of Life,' Phil. 4:3), writes to the Corinthians.[4]

'Brethren, in our thoughts of Jesus Christ we ought to conceive of Him as God, and the Judge of quick and dead. We ought not to cherish low thoughts of Him who is our Saviour; for if our thoughts of Him are low, we will hope for little at His hand.' This truth admits of wide application. A soul very deeply convinced of sin, or indeed convinced of sin at all as an awful reality, will find no object fit for its necessities but the person of God–man, associated with all he did. It was thus with a minister who lies buried in Bunhill Fields, Mr Bradford. He was for a time an Arian, but was awakened to feel that he must be born again, while writing a sermon on the words of Christ to Nicodemus. He felt sin in its power; he saw his sins to be innumerable, as well as inexpressibly heinous. 'And now,' says he, 'the first relief I felt was from the view that Jesus Christ was GOD. His deity I now saw as the ground of all my confidence.' No wonder! for it is there we see how

---

4.   In an Epistle still preserved and reckoned genuine.

the atonement could be sufficiently precious to avail for sinners such as we; it is only there we see how the Holy One could find a sacrifice for us pleasing and acceptable, and admitting of the widest application.

But, in cases where there is a tacit assent to the doctrine of the Person of Jesus, there is often a real and practical overlooking of it. Often, the deeply exercised soul looks at all else rather than the Living One Himself – thinking of his ways, purposes, work, but shutting its eyes on Himself. Now, let that soul be led for a time to deal with the Person, and the effect will be marvellous, if the Holy Spirit enables him to see who this Person is.

'How am I to cross that mountain?' says an anxious soul, pointing to the doctrine of electing love. 'How am I to find myself among the number of the elect?' 'And,' says another, 'if you cannot assure me that the blood of Christ was intended as much for me as for Peter or Paul, Mary Magdalene or Mary of Bethany, how can I rest on it?' Another, yet more bold, comes forward and declares that 'if Christ did not die alike for all men, and bear all sinners alike on His heart when He died, then there is no truth sufficient for a sinner seeking salvation to rest upon.'

Now, to all those travellers who would willingly (if they could) find out that there is no such mountain as electing love, because they fancy it is an insuperable one, we say at once, the Person of the Lord Jesus stands in front of that glorious mountain whose top touches heaven; and you have to do with His Person ere you set a foot on that mountain.

Our warrant for believing in Christ is simply this, that He cries to the children of men, 'To you, O men, I call.' And he bids them ALL come in the first place to HIMSELF. Come and see this Person (Prov. 8:4). 'If any man thirst, let him come unto me, and drink' (John 7:37). 'Come unto me, all ye that labour and are heavy laden' (Matt. 11:28) – ye that are toiling up that mountain with a load on your souls that almost crushes you at every step.

All your difficulties about election are thus set aside for the time – set aside until you have found Christ Himself, 'who will show you plainly of the Father' in due time. All your difficulties about election are in this manner transferred to Christ Himself, who it is (and not we) that must reconcile the universal call with His special love to His elect. Well, be content to leave the difficulty with Jesus; and meanwhile deal with a personal Saviour, not with words, and doctrines, and propositions. Say, if you will, 'Perhaps I am not elected, and if so it will be in vain for me to expect a place among His redeemed' – say this, if you will, but only go and see. Go to the Person of the Christ, and throw thyself at His feet.

Now, you do throw yourself at Christ's feet, when, letting alone for the time all these thoughts of election and the inquiry whether you are or are not in the Book of Life, you allow your soul to think of Christ Himself. Will Christ Himself refuse a coming sinner? He cannot; for it is written, 'Him that cometh to me I will in no wise cast out' (John 6:37). He will not say that He has not a price sufficient to pay for you. He will not say that the foundation is not broad enough for you to build on. He will not say that He has not love sufficient to lead Him to have compassion on you. You may not be able to make out from some of Christ's words whether or not there be room for you; but try Christ's heart – appeal to Him as one 'who receiveth sinners' – and tell Him that such a sinner are you.

Never forget the Syrophenician mother's dealing with the Lord. It is a case recorded as if on very purpose for such a state of soul as yours. This woman came, full of desire and hope, but was told, 'I am not sent but to the lost sheep of the house of Israel.' Was not this confronting her at once with the darkest shadow of the highest height of the mountain of Election? It seemed to say, 'There is no place for you.' It did not leave her an opening (as there is in your case) to say, 'Possibly I am in the number' – it seemed to deny that she was thought of at all. If ever there was a trying case it was here. But how did this woman act? She did not try to prove, as some do in our day, that there was not, and could not be, such a thing as special electing love – but she left that difficulty to be solved by the Lord Himself, and threw herself upon the Person of Jesus. She renewed her appeal to Himself, 'Lord, help me.' 'Truth, Lord, but the dogs (and such am I) under the table eat of the crumbs.' She probed His heart; she believed there were depths of mercies there; and she found she was right! She has left us a proof that when a sinner repairs to the Person of the living Saviour, that sinner is at once met by Him; and the gracious colloquy begins – 'Come now, let us reason together, saith the LORD' (Isa. 1:18); and it will end with nothing less than absolution, 'Though your sins have been as scarlet, they shall be as white as snow; though they have been red like crimson, they shall be as wool.' Believest thou this? In believing this, thy soul shall find acceptance with God; and in the same hour, thy Lord will let thee know that He had thee in His heart from eternity. It is thus that an anxious soul's stumbling on the difficulty of election may become a real advantage. It guides the soul away from a thing to a person. His first question now is not, What does Christ think of me? But, What am I to think of Christ? The traveller is confronted by the frowning mountain–height, and this leads him at once to discover, ere he climbs even one height, the Person to whose dwelling he imagined he must come by long and laborious efforts. Boldly encounter the question, 'Am I one of God's elect? Am I one given to Christ by the Father from all eternity?' It will lead you directly to the Person of Jesus, as the only mode of reaching a true and sure solution. It will send you not to the Book of Life, but to the Lamb who writes it; and in asking about Him, you find that He has singular love to sinners, and that 'He is able to save to the uttermost them that come unto God by him' (Heb. 7:25).[5]

---

5. It is thus in general that little children rest on Christ. With little theology, they know and feel that this is He who died for sinners. Their faith is like that of Old Testament saints; it is the sheep resting on the shepherd's shoulders, with little knowledge of how He saves them.

Is this not enough?

We may here take occasion to observe that a fresh view of His Person, especially in its human aspect, seems, from the Gospels, to be the Lord's way of removing the after fears of His own. We find that the Lord, when on earth, used to remove fear by revealing Himself. On that memorable night of storm, when wind and waves tossed the vessel, and darkness had spread its thickest veil over moon and stars, Jesus walked on the waters and approached them. They thought that it was 'a spirit' (Matt. 14:26), or angelic messenger (it might be some one of the 'ministering spirits'), was no consolation to men who at that hour were ready to perish, and who felt worthy to perish. They saw nothing in an angel's presence but what might remind them, by contrast, of their own unholiness; and they knew nothing of the depth of an angel's compassion. But no sooner did Jesus speak, 'IT IS I,' than there was a calm in their souls, such as the after–calm on the surface of the lake was but an emblem of: 'It is I!' I am here! was all He said. But they knew His heart as well as His hand. They knew His love to them, unworthy as they were. They knew His sinner–love – His love to men. And why should we not have this same remedy for our anxieties? The living Jesus – Jesus, full of human sympathies and divine glories!

It was so again after the Resurrection. In Luke 24:36-47, we read of the scene. The disciples had lately sinned, and were not as yet altogether at rest. When, therefore, one enters the Upper Room who seemed to be from the other side of the Veil, they are sore afraid – as if tidings from that side must be evil tidings to them, and as if a holy angel, even a holy ministering 'spirit,' must have been sent on some errand of reproof or judgment. But it was the Lord! and He lifted up His voice with the salutation, 'Peace' – man's salutation taken up by the God–man's lips into which grace is poured. And then He drew all their attention to His Person, as not that of an angel, but of one who had 'flesh and bones – that is, who had man's nature. He showed them 'hands and feet' – the hands that had so often touched the sick to heal them, and been laid on themselves to bless them; – the feet that for them had been weary on the highways of Judea and Galilee, and had got no rest till they touched the cold stone of Joseph's sepulchre. 'Why are ye troubled?' said He, as if to recall the night of the last supper: 'Let not your hearts be troubled' (John 14:1-26). 'And why do thoughts arise in your minds?'– thoughts or disputings as to who this was. He hastened yet farther to show them His true humanity – that He was the God–man, the Lord of glory, who put on their very nature; for He asked for fish and honey–comb, and did eat with them as a guest at their board.

No wonder that (Luke 24:35) they were so full of joy at the very possibility of His very self being there, so full that they could scarcely allow themselves to believe it. But they show us in what manner immediate calm is to be found; and true rest from anxiety; they show us the real removal of questionings and troubles, and the simple means of being filled with joy unspeakable. The streams from Lebanon furnish it all! The Person of the God–

man presents thoughts, and declares truths, and reveals feelings towards us, such as may well cause a soul to cry, 'All my springs are in thee!' He did not come saying, 'Peter, I love thee'; 'Bartholomew, I love thee,' 'And I love thee, Thaddeus,' 'And thee, Philip' – but He took a way which made all of them feel more than even if He had done and said this very thing, He presented among them Himself in His humanity! Lo! (as if He had said) Lo! I am among you, the Incarnate God, whose love has led me to be man's Redeemer. Handle me and see! Draw out of this well – wherein is love not only to you, Peter, and to you, Bartholomew, and to you, Thaddeus, and to you, Philip – but to 'a great multitude whom no man can number,' out of every kindred, and tongue, and people. Draw from this well and thirst no more.

'He that hath ears to hear let him hear.' To have rejected the Saviour – to have slighted Him – to have refused to make Him welcome, on the pretext of imagined difficulties, will be as the 'worm that never dies' to your soul! And further we say, to have received less than the Person of Him who died and rose again – to have been satisfied with mere propositions and statements, with mere doctrines and truths, instead of embracing in your heart the very Person to whom all these referred will be to you the 'worm that never dies' – a subject of endless regret in eternity, when regret is unavailing. You are like a man laying himself to repose on the bosom of a cloud, on the white down of the ocean's foam. Oh, the misery of the soul that is content with a shadow instead of substance! –

content with a vague belief that there was a sort of general love and mercy to all, and a kind of general vindication of righteousness and moral government, instead of taking the full, ample soul–filling and conscience–filling atonement, – salvation for him by means of such a personal substitute as the Lord Jesus, the Son of the Highest!

What is 'Wrath to come,' if, to avert it from sinners, the Lord Jehovah rose from His throne! But on the other hand, where is the possibility of perishing if a sinner accept Him who has come? Yonder is the baring of the Almighty's bosom, proclaiming, 'Yet there is room.' Yonder is an ocean–depth of love, which even Manasseh has not yet fathomed – yonder is an atmosphere of love to the height of which even Paul has never soared! And (herein indeed is love!) we may taste it, each for ourselves! It is the bosom on which even we may for ever rest.

4

HOW LOOKING TO THE PERSON OF CHRIST TENDS TO PROMOTE THE PEACE THAT PASSES UNDERSTANDING

No one could be supposed to have seen the Alps, if he tells you that all he saw was some rocky ridges of hills which his eye felt no strain in looking to. The Alps are not such hills; they tower to the clouds. Equally true it is that no one can be considered as having really seen sin, who never saw it to be very great; or to have got real rest to his soul, who has not seen the Saviour to be very great. Indeed, very great salvation is needed in order to give any true peace to a soul truly awakened; such salvation as is discovered when the soul discovers the Person of the Saviour. Then it sings, 'JAH JEHOVAH is my strength and song, and has become my salvation' (Isa. 12:2).

> In JAH JEHOVAH[1]
> is the Rock of ages (26:4).

---

1. These are the only passages where that particular combination occurs, 'Jah–Jehovah'; as if to gather up the fulness of Godhead-existence in one clause, when singing of Him who is our salvation. He from whom every drop of being came is mine!

Even one sin makes peace flee from the soul, as we see in the case of Adam and Eve. Even one sin fills the soul with suspicions of God and suggestions of fear. Of course, then, the conscience of every sinner abounds in materials for fear before God. Achan may be secure for a time, while his wedge of gold and his Babylonish garment remain hid in the tent; but let a hurricane from the howling wilderness shake the cords and canvas of his tent, threatening to blow aside the covering of his theft, and then he is full of alarm! Now, to the conscience of the sinner, every sin is like Achan's theft. There may be a present calm in the air, but who can promise that there shall not arise a stormy wind? A hurricane threatening to tear up the stakes of his earthly tabernacle? Who can engage that every sin shall not be laid bare? Who can give security that the sinner shall not in the twinkling of an eye be sisted at the bar of the Holy One? It is a small matter to say that, at present, all is at rest within. A city may be wrapt in slumber, and under the calm moon may seem as quiet as a cemetery; and yet the first beams of the morning sun may awake sleeping rebels, and witness the burst of revolutionary frenzy.

Every sin is secretly uttering to the man God's sentence of death; insinuating uneasy forebodings regarding coming wrath. Every sin mutters to the sinner something more or less distinct about having wronged God, and about God being too holy and just to let it slip from remembrance. And when the quickening Spirit is at work in the conscience, every sin cries loudly to the Lord for vengeance against him in whose heart it has its abode.

For such a state of soul only one thing can avail – namely, the discovery which the Spirit makes to the man in conversion, the discovery of Christ's full sacrifice for sin. Therein may be seen a propitiation as full and efficacious as conscience craves, because it was wrought out by Him who is God–man. Therein may be seen the whole Person of the Saviour presented to the soul as the object to be embraced, and that person associated with the merit of all He has done and suffered. Nay, more; every act and suffering of that glorious Person confronts the case of every sinner. Not only does He remedy the case of every individual sinner of all that 'multitude which no man can number,' but besides, He meets every individual sin, and applies out–poured life to each stain, to blot it out. This is exactly what was needed. If I see Him who is the atonement to be God–man, then I see an offering so vast, and so extensive in its applications, that every crevice of the conscience must be reached.

He is our peace, not by His death only, but by His life of obedience also, imputed to us. The more, therefore, we go into details with His Person (the Person of Him whose every act and agony has an infinite capability of application because of His being the God–man), then the more shall we see good reason why our peace through Him should be peace 'passing understanding' (Phil. 4:7). Let us exhibit some details of the kind we refer to – viz., His personal acts and sufferings meeting my personal disobedience and my personal desert of wrath.[2]

---

2. 'His humiliation expiates our pride; His perfect love atones for our ingratitude; His exquisite tenderness pleads for our insensibility' (JOHN NEWTON, Sermon I.).

I confess the sin of my nature, my original sin: 'Behold! I was shapen in iniquity, and in sin did my mother conceive me' (Ps. 51:5). But I see in Christ one who, while He was 'that Holy One,' was born to be holiness to others (Luke 1:35). His dying was fully sufficient to remove the guilt of my conception, and my connection with Adam; while His doing was holy from the womb. Behold! then, here am I in my substitute! My infancy without iniquity, nay, with actual purity, in the eye of Him who is well pleased with my Substitute.

I confess the sin of my childhood. My childhood and youth were vanity. But I find in Christ, God–man and my Substitute, deliverance from all this guilt. 'The child grew and waxed strong in spirit, filled with wisdom; and the grace of God was upon him' (Luke 2:40). I get all the positive merit of this childhood of my surety, full as it was of holy wisdom, and free from every taint of folly and thoughtlessness; and along with this I get the atoning merit of His death. And thus I present to God both satisfaction for the trespasses I have done in my childhood, and also obedience equivalent in full to what the law had, right even, then to expect or claim from me.

I confess more particularly the sin of my thoughts, 'Every imagination of the thoughts of my heart has been only evil continually' (Gen. 6:5). But I discover Him who not only by death perfected the atonement for me, but who also obeyed my obedience in the thoughts of the heart, saying, 'Thy law is within my heart' (in the midst of my bowels) (Ps. 40:8).

I confess the sin of my words, my idle words, my evil words. For it is written (Matt. 12:36), 'Every idle word that men shall speak, they shall give account thereof in the day of judgment.' But I find in this great atonement the penalty paid for my every idle word. I find, at the same time, the rendering of the obedience due by me, inasmuch as His mouth was a well of life, 'grace was poured into his lips' (Ps. 45:2), and men never heard Him utter aught but words of holiness.

I confess the sin of my duties: for example, the sin of my careless worship in the sanctuary. But I find my glorious Substitute worshipping for me in the synagogue. (Luke 4:16), 'He came to Nazareth, and as his custom was he went into the synagogue.' I find Him vindicating the honour of His Father in the temple–service. (John 2:16-17), 'Make not my Father's house an house of merchandise. And his disciples remembered that it was written, The zeal of thine house hath eaten me up.' His songs of praise, His deep attention to the written Word there read, His joining in the public prayers, all this He puts to my account, as if I had done it acceptably and done so always, while in the same moment, by His shed blood, He blots out every accusation against me for omissions and guilty acts.

I confess my prayerlessness in secret. It has grieved the Lord to the heart. But I find my surety 'rising a great while before day, and departing to a solitary place to pray' (Mark 1:35); or, 'continuing all night in prayer to God' (Luke 6:12). This He will impute to me, as if I had so prayed every day and night; at the same time plunging my sins of omission into the depths of the sea.

I confess and deplore heart–sins of various kinds. I lament instability of soul; my goodness is like the early dew. But He was 'the same yesterday, to–day, and for ever,' both God–ward and man–ward (Heb. 13:8). I feel hardness of heart. But He imputes to me His own tenderness, and reckons to my account His own yearnings of soul for the glory of His Father. I am stubborn; but He can say, 'The LORD GOD opened mine ear, and, I was not rebellious, neither turned away backwards' (Isa. 50:5). In me is guile, but 'in His mouth was no guile found' (1 Pet. 2:22). And thus there is ready not only the warp of satisfaction for transgression, but also the woof of rendered obedience.

Let me still go on a little in this application of my Lord's active and passive righteousness. Do I feel my soul in anguish, because of indulging ambitious projects, seeking to be somewhat? I find Him 'not seeking His own glory' (John 8:50): and this fold of His robe He will cast over me, while by His blood He washes me from all my self–seeking.

I have pleased myself. But of Him it is testified, 'He pleased not Himself' (Rom. 15:3). I have sought my own will. But He could declare before the Father and to men, 'I seek not mine own will, but the will of the Father which hath sent me' (John 5:30). And thus has He fully given the very form of obedience that I have omitted to render. He gave what I withheld; and He will give it for me, at the same time that my guilt in withholding it is hidden in His blood.

I have been worldly. I have loved 'the world and the things that are in the world' (1 John 2:15); not only the objects it presents, but the very place itself, in preference to place and things wherein the direct presence of God might be enjoyed. But He did not. 'He was not of the world' (John 17:14). He never had any of its treasure; it is doubtful if He ever possessed or handled any of its money; we are sure He had nowhere to lay His head. The world hated Him, 'because He testified that the works thereof were evil' (John 7:7). And all this He has at hand to impute to me, while He washes me from guilt.

I have been often double-minded. His eye was always single. 'I have glorified Thee' (John 17:4) was always true of Him. I have been inconsistent; but even Satan could find 'nothing in Him' (John 14:30). And He could challenge His foes, 'which of you convinceth me of sin?' (John 8:46).

My pride and haughtiness have need of One who was 'meek and lowly.' And such I find in Him; and I find Him calling me to come to Him as such, and use Him (Matt. 11:29).

If I have backslidden, yet my Surety's course was truly like 'the shining light, that shineth more and more unto the perfect day' (Prov. 4:18). 'He increased in wisdom and stature, and in favour with God and man' (Luke 2:52). Instead of lukewarmness ever on any occasion appearing in Him, such was His zeal for men's salvation that, at one time, friends stood by and said, 'He is beside himself'

(Mark 3:21); and at another, His disciples were irresistibly led back to the words of the Psalmist, 'The zeal of thine house hath eaten me up' (John 2:17). Now, all this active righteousness in Him is for my use. He will throw over me this other fold of His robe, as well as apply His infinitely precious death – and thus no one shall ever be able to accuse me of backsliding, God accepting my Surety's work for me.

I have grieved the Spirit. But oh, how Christ honoured Him! Such blessed things He said of Him! 'The Comforter,' 'the Spirit of truth,' 'the Holy Spirit,' were names which He applied to Him; and Himself had been led by Him in delighted acquiescence. 'Jesus being full of the Holy Ghost, returned from Jordan, and was led by the Spirit into the wilderness' (Luke 4:1). He has something here to present instead of my provocations; and what He has, He will use for me. Only let me know the treasures hid in His Person, and my consolation must abound.

I have been unthankful; but oh! how my Surety abounded in thanksgivings, – thanksgivings for food, – thanksgivings for the Gospel revealed to babes, – thanksgivings for the communion table, because it proclaimed His dying for us. Herein I find obedience to a law I broke, the law of gratitude – while in the sacrifice of Calvary, I find expiation for my guilty ingratitude.

I think upon my unconcern for souls. And I find the remedy for that iniquity in Him whose heart burned 'to seek and save that which was lost,' and who plunged into the sea of wrath in order to redeem – for every step in

His atonement has in it something of obedience as well as satisfaction.

Oh, inconceivable fulness for us in Him! whatever be the special sin which our conscience at any moment is feeling. Only let us ever keep Christ Himself in view, Christ clothed to the foot in that garment of active and passive righteousness.

It is thus we get the sea, with all its multitudinous waves[3] (Isa. 48:18, 'righteousness like the waves of the sea'), to flow up every creek and sweep round every bay. His Person being such, His work completely fits into the soul's necessities. And all this is so great, that not only does it affect us negatively – not only does this full view of Christ remove every tremor from the soul – it works besides into the heart a positive bestowal of bliss.

It is as sometimes in nature when every breath of wind is so lulled asleep that not a leaf moves on the bough of any tree; the sun is shedding his parting ray on the still foliage; and the sea rests as if it had become a pavement of crystal. This is peace in nature. Your heart feels, amid such a scene, not only the absence of whatever might create alarm or disquiet, but the presence also of some elements of positive enjoyment, as if there were an infusion of bliss

3. There is a wave of it for ministerial failures; for He never failed, but could appeal to His Father, 'I have declared thy faithfulness, and thy salvation' (Ps. 40:10). His Shepherd's heart and work cover over ours. And so let a teacher repair to Him for the hiding of sins in teaching. 'In the day time he was teaching in the temple' (Luke 21:37). 'I ever taught in the synagogue and in the temple' (John 18:20).

in the scene. Now, infinitely more is this the case in the kingdom of grace. The presence of Christ in the heart (the Spirit there testifying of Christ) lulls fear to sleep; and while He makes disquiet almost an impossibility, never fails to bring in positive delight and bliss. There is something in it to 'keep the heart and mind' (garrison, and so preserve secure) (Phil. 4:7). And what is this positive element but the real outbreathing of direct friendship and love for Him whose heart we now know? He removes the barriers out of the way and out of sight, in order to bring in Himself with all His love – Himself rich in all affections and bowels of mercy. And is not this the true 'healing' of the 'hurt'? Was not the 'hurt,' our separation from the Holy One, caused by sin? Is not this the 'healing', then, our return to fellowship with Him?

It is worthwhile asking, in every case of apparent peace, whether or not this positive element exists. Is there not only the absence of dread and a calmness in looking towards the Holy One, but, in addition to this, is there direct enjoyment of Him who gives the peace? The work of Christ, if seen apart from His Person, may give freedom from dread of wrath, but it can scarcely impart that positive delight in His restored friendship, which alone 'keepeth the heart and mind.'

'He is our Peace,' says Paul, in Ephesians 2:14. And when, in Philippians 4:7, he spoke of His peace keeping the heart and mind ('the thoughts'– in the original), he said it was 'by Christ Jesus.' Was not Paul here directed by the Spirit to insert this clause in order to fix our eye on the Person who is our peace – the true 'Jehovah–shalom?' (Judg. 6:24). And is not the reason of this to be found in the fact that in proportion as we see the Person, our soul's peace spreads and deepens? Certainly, all who have tried it find this to be the case. The more they know of Him, the more complete is their souls' rest. It is shallow peace (if it be indeed the 'peace of God' at all), when the Person of the Peacemaker is not directly realised.

And now, seeing we have such advantages above Old Testament saints, who saw the Person so dimly, are there not duties and responsibilities resulting? 'The darkness is past and the true light now shineth' (1 John 2:8). Therefore (says John) there is for you 'A new commandment.' He seems to mean that the increase of light has given force to every demand for obedience; and especially that the appearing of this Light, the Person Jesus, has brought with it peculiar motives to obedience. May we not say that if we get such peace in Jesus Christ, and have Himself to calm our souls, the Lord may well expect at our hands a higher style of obedience than in former days?

Peace has its responsibilities – such peace through such a Redeemer, has no common responsibilities. We are freed from burdens in order to work for God – we are fully justified in order to be the more fully sanctified. Carry this kind of peace with you everywhere, and you cannot fail everywhere to show that you are with Jesus; for it is Himself realised that gives it. Your claim to real peace implies your seeing Christ Himself, and enjoying His fellowship. If so, then you may well be expected to show likeness to Jesus; for 'he that walketh with wise men shall be wise' (Prov. 13:20). Your peace will be characterised by purity, as all ever is that comes from God (James 3:17), and as all must be that is the direct effect of an eye fixed on 'God manifest in the flesh.' Your peace 'in Jesus Christ' will keep you daily at His side, engaged in His work, guided by His look, satisfied with His smile, living to do His will. Who could have his eye on that Saviour continually, and there see 'peace in heaven' toward himself, and yet, at the same time, turn his feet into the by–paths of unholiness?

Were your peace gotten or maintained by looking at an act of your own – viz., your having once believed, or having done the thing called believing, then possibly you might be at peace, and yet after all not walk with God. But in as much as true Scriptural peace is gotten and maintained by the sinner's eye resting at the moment on the Person of Him who is our peace – on the person of Jehovah–shalom[4] – it is not possible to be at peace and yet at the same time willingly wander from fellowship with the Holy One. Christ, our Peace–maker, walks among us wherever is to be found anything 'true, or honest, or just, or lovely, or of good report' – wherever is to be seen 'any virtue or any praise' (Phil. 4:8).

And he who has peace by having his eye on Christ cannot enjoy this peace without being led at the same moment to these walks of Christ. Hence it is that Paul writes to the Philippian Church – to Lydia, and the Jailor,

---

4.　Judges 6:24, 'Jehovah is peace'; like 1 John 4:8, 'God is Love.' It is at the altar of sacrifice that 'Jehovah is peace.'

and Euodias, and Syntyche, and Clement – that 'the God of peace would be with them' while they pursued these objects (Phil. 4:8-9). If they were found at any time wandering from these holy paths, it would be a sufficient sign to them (as it will be to us also), that they had for the time taken off their eyes from Him who was their peace – and so, ere they were aware, had lost the enjoyment of that deep, profound peace, which 'keepeth the heart and mind.'

5

HOW LOOKING TO THE PERSON TENDS TO ADVANCE HOLINESS IN THE SOUL

'Sanctify them by the truth' was our Lord's prayer; but it is truth in connection with Himself. For, separate from Him, doctrines 'have no living power, but are as waters separated from the fountain; they dry up, or become a noisome puddle, or as a beam interrupted from its continuity with the sun is immediately deprived of light.'[1]

There is an expressive type in the old economy that bears on this subject. The cherubim (emblems of the redeemed) stood upon the mercy–seat or lid of the Ark – that lid, or mercy–seat, on which the blood was seventimes sprinkled every atonement day. In this manner is set forth the soul's resting on the work of Christ; for here is His shed blood, and the feet of the cherubim touch that blood. But, at the same time, notice that they stood

---

1.   For further reading from John Owen on the person of Christ see: Owen, John, *The Person of Christ: Declaring a Glorious Mystery – God and Man* (Ross-Shire: Christian Focus Publications, 2016).

not on the blood alone, but on the mercy–seat – a part of that Ark which altogether was typical of Christ Himself, the depositary or treasure–chest of all our blessings. Thus they exhibited rest on the Person as well as on the work of Christ. Again, the cherubim looked down upon the blood that lay on the mercy–seat, but their look was not less fully directed towards the mercy–seat itself, and the Ark too. These symbolic figures of the redeemed spread out their wings over the blood, but not over that alone, but at least as fully over the mercy–seat and Ark – a significant action, expressive of their regarding it as worthy of care – nay, as being to them what to the mother–bird her brood is in the nest. The wings were spread forth on either side, as if purposely to show that the whole of the Ark was their care, the object of their solicitude and their delight.

Perhaps there was still more signified in their connection with that Ark. They not only stood upon it, and leant their whole weight on it, but they were also joined to it. For they formed one piece with the mercy–seat, which was the upper part of the Ark, and which was all of gold. Not content with representing them as ever gazing on this object, the Lord set forth their union to Himself who is the mercy–seat – union to Him in His glorified state (for they and it were of gold), sharing in all the fruits of His finished work and begun glory.

Union to Christ's Person is a fact in the case of every believer, and ought therefore to be a constant subject of meditation to every believer. Now, this union realised leads to a realising of the Person. Hence, in the Lord's

Supper, it is always important for the communicant to ask, with Paul, 'The cup of blessing which we bless, is it not the communion of the blood of Christ? The bread which we break, is it not the communion of the body of Christ? (1 Cor. 10:16). That ordinance, so rich in blessing and in blessed suggestions, is fitted always to bring us back to a fresh and present realising of the Person of Jesus, by bringing us to a remembrance of our union to that Person. Can we think of union to Him, and not go on to ask, Who is this to whom I am united? Who is this that is my husband? Who is this that is far more mine than the husband is the wife's? What is His heart? What is His hand of might? Where are His possessions? Where are the proofs of His love? Are His glories bursting on my view?

The great truth, which the Ark in the Old Testament, and the Lord's Supper in the New, is so well fitted to keep before us, has been the object of endeavour and pursuit (if not always of attainment) to all believers who have been found growing in holiness. In the latter days of the life of Howell Harris, of Wales, the intent gaze of his soul on the Person of Jesus is as remarkable, as was his intent look to the terrors of Sinai in earlier days. He writes to a friend (Lett. 43), 'One view of Him, in His eternal Godhead, and so of the infinity of His Person, love, obedience, and suffering, is worth millions of worlds.' In another (Lett. 52), 'How is it with all you? Doth the veil wear off, and doth the glory of a crucified Saviour appear brighter and brighter? Oh, my brother, that Man is indeed the eternal God. What views doth He give vile me of Himself!

He shines brightly like the sun at noon! Oh, what heart of stone would not melt to see the eternal God lying in a manger, sweating and tired, wearing His thorny crown, not opening His mouth, because He bare our sin and shame? Go on, my dear brother, and be bold in the great mystery of God become man.'

Undoubtedly, it mellows and matures the character of saints to be much occupied with their Lord's Person; but as undoubtedly, it quickens their sense of obligation, and keeps alive love and gratitude, to be thus ever in contact with a personal Saviour. Ideas, however noble, may leave our souls comparatively dry, and they will always leave us infinitely less affected in our conscience, than when we meet our God in His personality.[2]

Now, while all believers do in some measure deal with a personal Christ, yet all do not seek to extend their experience of it; although the more this is done, the more fervent, and mild, and calm will all holiness be in their souls; for then they take it fresh from the spring, and that spring is the calm, deep soul of Jesus. There will be a difference in the tone of their life, and the fulness of their conformity to the image of their Lord, in proportion as their eye rests more or less frequently on His Person. Indeed, so much is this the case, that we are inclined to think that Peter referred very specially to this style

---

2. Trench, in one of his Hulsean Lectures, puts the case thus: 'Oh, how great the difference between submitting ourselves to a complex of rules, and casting ourselves upon a beating heart' (P. 122).

of experience, when he was inspired to write, 'Grow in grace and in the knowledge of our Lord and Saviour Jesus Christ' (2 Pet. 3:18).

Many saints seem to be little aware how much of grace there is in the knowledge of the Person of Jesus. It would singularly benefit some of these, who have lived much on what they know about Jesus, to try for a week the more blessed and fruitful way of dealing directly with Himself. There are treasures in the Person of Him whose doctrines they believe, if only they could use them. A great philosopher says, on another subject, what we may accommodate to this – 'A man may believe in the work and Person of Christ for twenty years, and only in the twenty–first – in some great moment – is he astonished at the rich substance of his belief – the rich warmth of this naphthaspring.' He adds to his ideas a person, and exchanges knowledge about a truth for knowledge of Him that is true – yes, exchanges opinions for a deep joy in the Living One, a joy which nothing earthly gave nor can destroy.

By this looking to the Person, the believer's holiness, or growth in grace, is advanced in a threefold way. For this looking to the Person leads – 1. To communion; 2. To a realising of His life for us; 3. To imitation – all which conform the soul to His likeness.

1. Communion with Him is one result, and a sanctifying result. When we dwell on the Saviour's Person, we are in His company. Faith places us by His side, and shows us His glory, until what we see makes our heart burn

within us. We are virtually put in the position of disciples walking by His side, witnessing His excellences, basking in the radiance of grace and truth from His countenance, hearing His words. Now, this contemplation of Him is transforming in its effects; 'Beholding the glory of the Lord, we are changed into the same image' (2 Cor. 3:18). This is the plan which the Holy Spirit takes in conforming us to Christ's image. In this way, He daguerreotypes on our prepared hearts the likeness of Him whom we look to.

This communion was carried on very constantly by Samuel Rutherford while in exile, hour after hour. The day seemed short while so engaged; and thus it was he exhorted a friend: 'I urge upon you a nearer communion with Christ, and a growing communion. There are curtains to be drawn by in Christ that we never saw, and new foldings of love in Him. I despair that ever I shall win to the far end of that love; there are so many plies in it. Therefore, dig deep – and set by as much time in the day for Him as you can – He will be won by labour.'

But is it not intimated to us, by there being such a book as 'the Song of Songs,' that the Lord desires far more of our communion with Him than we generally relish? Was not that Song of Songs written to teach us this dealing with Himself? It was given to the Church in Old Testament days, when His Person as yet was dimly seen; for so great was His desire for this personal converse with us, He would teach it even then. How much more now should it be our occupation, when we see the Bridegroom, and know Him as revealed by Himself? Is there much of that tender love in the present day? Are there many of His own who are saying to Him, 'Let me kiss him with the kisses of his love' (Song 1:2) – using that figure for want of any other adequate terms? Are many telling Him, 'I am sick of love. If ye find my beloved, tell him that I am sick of love?' (Song 5:8). Have we at all adequately realised our privilege of holding 'fellowship' with Him, as a man speaketh to His friend? 'Truly,' said John, 'our fellowship is with the Father, and with his Son, Jesus Christ' (1 John 1:3). There was here personal intercourse, the soul of disciples with the soul of the master. There was no doubt, in spirit, all the reality of the converse exhibited in the Song of Songs, and realised by each disciple in the Upper Room.

2. Thus living on the Son of God personally leads us to realise His life for us. By His life for us is meant His manner of spending for us the three–and–thirty years He lived on earth, as well as His continually using for us 'the power of His endless life,' now in heaven. All that is associated with that Person, we cannot but seek to call to mind. Every notice of His former walk on earth we eagerly read, that we may thereby know His heart, He being 'the same yesterday, to–day, and for ever.'

All the records of His sympathy with us in our misery, every trait of His tender pity, whatever indicates His thoughts, we peruse with untiring fondness – returning to the meditation again and again with as engrossing an interest as at first. On this account, the four gospels possess indescribable attractions; for there it is we glean the finest wheat – glimpses of His glory and grace, human and divine.

What He did, what He said, what He suffered, what He felt, what He thought; how He was silent, how He spoke; His journeyings, His places of rest; the words He used in healing, the look, the prayer, the touch, the command, the call – all have an engrossing interest, because God–man is there. And then, not less, the outgushings of grace and truth, in the outpouring of His soul unto death, and in the resurrection–victory, and in the discoveries of the same heart toward us when His exaltation was begun, and His robe of righteousness had been waved with acceptance before the Father.

But still more. We follow Him as 'He feeds among the lilies.' We try to feel His heart beating for us in heaven; and just as one walking with Aaron, the High Priest, could not but see the breast–plate with its names, so we cannot fail to see that this Jesus bears the names of His own on His heart. We find it written, 'We shall be saved by his life' (Rom. 5:10). We go up to Him, and find His love as intense, and His merit as fresh, as when He rose from the tomb. We realise Him as 'every moment watering His vine' – interceding and obtaining daily grace for us. His life above is a life of love, no less than was His life below. Behold, how He thinks upon us night and day! Not content with putting into our hand the cup of blessing on the day of our conversion, He takes care to keep it in our possession and to keep us from spilling its new wine. He remembers still how He hid us in the cleft on that day when we flew as trembling doves to the rock; and He keeps us as safely hid as ever. Not only did He once blot out our sins, but

He is employed in seeing that the writing never reappear. He once put on us a robe of righteousness: He every hour continues to keep it on us, in spite of blasts from earth and hell. He once plunged all our sins in the depth of the sea. He still appears for us in the presence of God, keeping the deep tide that buries these sins from ever ebbing. He once acquitted us and gained us honour far greater than was gained by Mordecai before Ahasuerus: He is every day still engaged in preventing us ever falling into disgrace.

In this manner, we feel our acceptance and the communication of blessing to us fresh each day, through Him who is our life; and so nothing in our religion grows old, and none of our reasons for close dependence on Him are past and out of date; nay, our everyday life is in a manner a daily repetition of the day of our first conversion. By this view, a daily impulse is given to our walk with God. Is not this what we need for continual progress? And is not this the Spirit's manner of watering the roots of the plants of grace?

And at the same time, as a man much in Aaron's company would see on his person and garments the anointing oil, so in our interceding Lord we see the Holy Spirit dwelling without measure. We see Him with the 'seven Spirits of God,' and this all for us. Our eye, resting on the Person of Jesus, discovers therein a reservoir of all holiness for our souls, inasmuch as He has the Spirit without measure. And so we learn to take from Him 'that other Comforter,' who delights to glorify the Saviour, and who is Himself infinite love and loveliness. What a sight for a soul like ours! 'The Spirit of wisdom and revelation,' dwelling in Him whom we long to know more and more. We read, in a manner, on His vesture and on His thigh, 'Thou hast received gifts for men, yea, for the rebellious also!' (Ps. 68:18).

3. But further, there is Imitation – imitation of Him we look upon. Long ago, Origen wrote: 'Faith brings with it a spiritual communion with Him in whom one believes; and hence a kindred disposition of mind which will manifest itself in works – the object of faith being taken up into the inner life.'[3] We do not look only on His wounds, but also on His holy steps; and we not only look, but by the sure leading of that Spirit who shows us what we see, we at the same moment seek to imitate. For the inmost soul is moved.[4]

Looking much to Jesus in His person, we instinctively (so to speak) copy what we see. Indeed, real holiness is simply the 'Imitation of Christ,' after He has washed us, and in the depth of His atoning grace left us without guilt. It is grateful imitation, not the imitation of those who are working for life. Much in the presence of our Benefactor who so loved us, we would fain resemble Him in our character and state of mind, and so we seek to copy what is imitable in His ways, and in all He manifested of

---

3. Neander's Church History, Volume 2, p. 283.

4. The soul whose sight all–quickening grace renews
    Takes the resemblance of the good she views;
    As diamonds stript of their opaque disguise
    Reflect the noonday glory of the skies.
    (COWPER, Charity)

Himself while redeeming us. We are led to desire (as Paul recommends in Phil. 2:5) to be filled with the 'mind that was in Christ,' that mind which shone out so attractively as He bore the cross and drank the cup to the dregs – for the Apostle Peter (2:21-24) exhorts us to observe even His example while hanging on the cross as containing some matter for imitation, some footsteps for us to walk in.

In this same way, true and steady looking to Christ's Person would, by the Spirit's teaching, lead us into the experience of that 'charity' which is described in 1 Corinthians 13:4-7. It is said to have these fourteen qualities, each one of which is best learned by beholding it in Christ, the original.

a. 'Charity suffereth long.' Where was this love illustrated if not in our Lord when He refused to bring down fire on the rejecters of His grace – stretched out His hands all day to rebels – bore mockery, blasphemy, wrong, the scourge, the crown of thorns, the reed, the blindfolding napkin, and the cross itself?

b. Charity is 'kind'. And who so truly kind as Jesus, crying with loud voice, 'It is finished,' and bringing us life in the moment of His own death – proclaiming the sweetest news with the vinegar at His lips! When was Joseph so kind to his brethren? Who ever so heaped coals of fire upon an enemy's head?

c. If ever we are to learn the love that 'envieth not,' we must see it in Him who desired nought for Himself, but disinterestedly and unceasingly sought to make our condition better, happier, greater. If our Priest, who wore the robe without a seam, had worn the priestly mitre on His brow, on it would have been written, 'More blessed to give than to receive.' He interfered with none of our comforts, not even in thought: it was only with our miseries. Let us drink in His unenvious, unselfish love, leaving our fellow-men all the true good they have, anxious only to make them have as much as ourselves.

d. Looking to His Person again, we see 'charity vaunteth not itself.' In Him is no ostentation, no parade of His doings. We read all the gospels through, and never find His love put itself forward for show. He does not clothe the naked and tell that He has done it; or relieve a Lazarus, and then remind the man that He has done him a favour; or heal, and proclaim His rare skill. Even His redeeming love is rather set within our view in His actions and agonies, as in so many wells whence we may draw, than pressed on us in words. Nor did He upbraid, or taunt, or shout haughty triumph over a soul subdued and forgiven – so little of parade had He. His is a Father's love to a prodigal son, too glad to gain the opportunity of pouring out itself on its object. Where shall we learn unostentatious love, if not here?

e. Or are we to learn the love that 'is not puffed up' – that has no inward self-gratulation, no self-complacent thought of its own magnanimity in the deed so kindly done? It is to be learned surely by looking to Him who was satisfied in gaining His gracious object, in finding scope for love. No look or tone of His ever made His benefactions disagreeable to those who received them; for

His was a charity that despised none, being the great love of God (Job 36:5). If we will learn holy love to others, let us learn it at Christ's holy love to us; as painters take for models the masterpieces of the best artists and copy them line by line.

f. Behold His love, and see how charity 'doth not behave itself unseemly.' You see a delicate propriety and a fine attention to the feelings in Christ's dealings of love. No rudeness, no harshness, no indiscretion; nothing mean, nothing unpolite; time, place, and persons were all consistently and tenderly considered. Even in this, the Righteous Servant 'dealt prudently.' With what tender delicacy, and yet determined love, did He deal with the woman of Samaria, till at last He had withdrawn the veil and confronted her conscience with her five husbands and the one that bore that name still! Even to Judas, in the hour of dark treachery, love could say, 'Friend, wherefore art thou come?' Never was there extravagant demonstration; never the shadow of affectation. There is seemly love to be learned in its perfection here, but only here, only in Jesus Himself.

g. And need we dwell on the charity 'that seeketh not her own'? In the life and death of Him, who 'was servant of all,' we see this love to the full – the seeking love of God – the love that sought us and ours.

h. The same love is seen 'not easily provoked.' See it personified in Him who stands there and groans over the city, 'Oh, Jerusalem, Jerusalem, how often would I have gathered thy children together!' (Matt. 23:37). No bitter wrongs ever drew forth a hasty word, or angry look, or revengeful blow. They spat in His face, they plucked off His hair, they smote Him with the palms of their hand, they put on the purple robe – but it drew forth only love.

i. His love was charity that 'thinketh no evil' – that never had a passing thought of injuring its worst foes, nor imagined them worse than they showed themselves to be. His were thoughts of peace, and not of evil, towards the men that crucified Him. 'If thou hadst known, even thou!' (Luke 19:42).

j. It is at His side we see and learn 'love rejoiceth not in iniquity, but rejoiceth in the truth.' The good of those whom He loved He sought not to advance by any unholy gratification. His love was such as felt grieved at seeing its objects seeking happiness in ways not good and true. It had no joy in seeing iniquity anywhere, far less seeing it have place in the hearts of friends, however pleasing and fascinating that iniquity might be. The truth was what His love rejoiced in. Hence, His love led him to protest and war against sinful pleasures and pursuits: for His love was no Eli–like fondness. It was love that would not give to those whom it embraced a cup in which one drop of gall was mingled, however much they thirsted. Where else shall we learn charity like this?

k. And then in Him we see love which 'beareth all things' – endures trouble for others, and takes on itself the task of covering from view what is wrong.

l. This love, too, is love that 'believeth all things.' Yes, His love was a love ever ready to confide in its objects, ready to trust Matthew as soon as he was called, making him an apostle, and then an evangelist – ready to trust Peter, after his fall, bidding him 'feed His sheep' – not suspicious and distrustful. Oh, to learn from Him such generous love! Surely it is well for us to keep much company with Him in whom it dwells.

m. His love 'hoped all things.' It was like the love of a friend, who, sitting by the death–bed of one whom he loves, hopes on still, even when all physicians have given up hope – hopes because he loves so much and wishes what he hopes for. Such was the love of Jesus; not easily giving up its object – not soon cutting down its barren fig–trees (Luke 13:6-9). More of His love would make our life more perseveringly devoted to the good of others, however slight were the symptoms of success. And it is this we need in our day! And once more:

n. His, indeed, was the charity that 'endured all things,' which did not faint in its pursuit, nor was baffled by difficulties. 'Many waters could not quench His love, nor could the floods drown it.' Oh, to drink in this love – this holy charity! finding it all in the Saviour's Person.

> Such was the portrait an Apostle drew,
> The bright original was one he knew;
> Heaven held his hand –
> The likeness must be true.[5]

---

5. COWPER, Charity.

But the tendency to imitate the person whom we love, and with whom we oft personally converse, extends to the feelings as well as actions. We drink deep into his sorrows and his joys.

The Spirit of truth shows us 'the Man of Sorrows' and lifting up a little of the veil from such an hour as that which heard the cry, 'Eli! Eli!' discovers to us the unknown anguish which was borne as the wrath due to us. This woe, of course, we are not asked to bear, though into it we are ever to desire to look; but in His other sorrows there is much by sympathising with which we may be made to drink in His holiness. One of the sorrows that made Him cry, 'Oh, that I had wings like a dove' (Ps. 55:4-6), was the sight of a man's corruption. Into this feeling, the soul that walks by the side of Jesus tries to enter. If, again, another source of sorrow to Christ was man's misery, so that He groaned in spirit at the sight (John 11:33), into this the companion of Jesus tries to enter. If another was the prospect of the doom overhanging sinners, with this, too, the believer sympathises, seeking to climb the Mount of Olives, and to stand with Jesus weeping over the guilty city (Luke 19:41). If Jesus is seen grieved over the fewness of the coming ones, 'Where are the nine?' (Luke 17:17), or is heard expressing sorrowful surprise at the slow progress of His own (Luke 24:25), or if He watches like a sparrow alone (Ps. 102:6-7), or, 'as an owl in the desert, as the pelican in the wilderness,' content with His Father's sympathy – in all this the soul that loves the company of 'the Man of Sorrows' seeks to share. And by this means the Holy Ghost pours the melted soul into the mould of Christ's heart. Or, if it be the joys of the Man of Sorrows that he is tracing out, in these, too, he seeks to be like Him. One of Christ's joys – one brook by the way, of which He drank – was the certainty that the Father's will was done (Luke 10:21); a second was the consciousness that He Himself was doing the Father's will (John 4:34); a third was the presence of the Father felt around Him (Acts 2:25-26); a fourth, the conversion of sinners (Luke 15); a fifth, the growth of faith in His own (Matt. 8:10); and a sixth, the hope of the reward (Heb. 12:2-3). In all these the growing believer, making Christ Himself his friend and divine companion, seeks to sympathise. He would fain be like Him whom he so loves.

There is something pleasant in noticing how Peter learnt to imitate his Lord by being so much in His company. When he goes to heal Dorcas (Acts 9:40-41) he put all out that wept and wailed, just as his Master did (Mark 5:37), and then the words, 'Tabitha, arise,' are brief, yet authoritative as his Master's 'Talitha, cumi' (Mark 5:41). So also he lifts up the lame man at the Beautiful Gate by the right hand (Acts 3:7), just as he had seen his Lord do (Mark 1:31) at Capernaum to his relative in her fever. Even so in greater things, the disciple falls into his Master's way and manner. Read his Epistles, and you see that, walking with the wise, he becomes wise; walking with the Gracious One, he becomes gracious; walking with Him who is holy, he becomes holy; walking with incarnate love and mercy, he becomes loving and merciful.

Among the friends of Alexander the Great, there was one named Hephaestion. It was said in regard to this man that he was 'A lover of Alexander' – none could doubt that man's personal affection for him. There was at the same time another friend, Oraterus, who seemed equally warm in heart and devotedness. It was, however, more because of the benefits conferred on him by one so exalted and great than from personal attachment – and hence he was said to be 'A lover of the King.' Which of these two most resembled their master in character? All history tells us it was Hephaestion, he who so loved the Person. And even so shall it be with the saint who dwells more on the Person of Immanuel than upon His gifts. The latter will be what was said of Peter (somewhat deprecatingly) by some of the ancients, 'A lover of Christ,' while the former will be what was said most truly of John, 'A lover of Jesus' – and, like John, will bear close resemblance to his Lord in every peculiar trait.

6

HOW THIS LOOKING TO THE PERSON AFFECTS OUR VIEWS OF DEATH AND OUR HOPE OF THE LORD'S SECOND COMING

In proportion as the soul advances in grace, its state coincides with that of the apostle, 'I am in a strait betwixt two, having a desire to depart and to be with Christ, which is far better; nevertheless to abide in the flesh is more needful for you' (Phil. 1:23-24). But at the same time that soul, if truly apostolic in its holiness, can add, 'Not that we would be unclothed, but clothed upon, that mortality might be swallowed up of life' (2 Cor. 5:4). It desires resurrection–bliss most of all, while, at the same time, it yearns after the lesser bliss of immediately passing into glory.

1. The main, and, indeed, the only, attraction of the intermediate state is this – there the redeemed see the Lord Jesus. He Himself is with them, and this is their heaven. In Revelation 6:9, the 'souls under the altar' are, undoubtedly, in this state; they are not represented in the glory of their resurrection state, as chapter 7:15-17, and

some passages may seem to set forth. These souls are at the altar, where they have taken up their station in order to cry for justice being done on the earth, as well as in order to show that justice is satisfied as to themselves; and there they are met by one who gives them 'white robes,' and who tells them they are to 'rest for a season'; leading them away to recline in their white robes on those couches of rest of which Isaiah (57:2) has told us. This is all we see of their outward bliss; but we cannot fail to notice that the 'rest' here, and in Revelation 14:13, is the continuation of the same 'rest' that their Lord from the very first spoke of giving (Matt. 11:28). It seems to be, like Lazarus in Abraham's bosom (Luke 16:22), a reclining with the Lord Jesus in view – reclining at a feast with the eye fixed on Jesus in the midst.

The moment a saint departs, he is 'with Christ.' This we read in Philippians 1:23, and, as we have already said, this 'being with Christ' is the essence of the bliss of that intermediate state, and is really all we know about it. The spirit of the departing one is received by Jesus (Acts 7:59); angels may receive it as it leaves the body (Luke 16:22), but they are not long of delivering it safe to their Lord. In His presence it rests, the sum of all its employments and its enjoyments being the sight and fellowship of the Lord Jesus. Nothing more is told us; for it would appear to be the design of the Lord to keep our eye on the Person of the beloved Son, as much on entering that unseen world as while here, and as much when arrived there as at entering.

'Blessed are the dead that die in the Lord.' They rest with Him, and see His face. They are gone to that 'mountain of myrrh and hill of frankincense' (Song 4:6), where Jesus Himself sits – at the right hand of the Father – and on the slopes of that hill they rest most pleasantly, beholding Him, and enjoying fellowship with Him, and waiting with Him for the daybreak and the flight of shadows. They are said to be 'in paradise' (Luke 23:43), the name appropriated to some part of the glorious heavens where the throne of God is seen – appropriated to it because of being the special spot where the children of the Second Adam are gathered together. As paradise was an inner part of Eden (Gen. 2:8), so is this abode of the redeemed an inner part of heaven. Perhaps it is the same as New Jerusalem. (Rev. 21:10) But at any rate, does not that name tell us of a place where God, as before the Fall, once more communes with men? It seems to say that the happy souls that dwell there, in light and love, are like unfallen Adam in his paradise – their chiefest joy being to hear the voice of the Lord God, to hear Him who is the Word of God.

We infer, then, that love to the Person of Jesus, and delight therein, is the state of mind nearest to that of those who have departed and are with Him. We are never more in sympathy with the saints departed than when rapt in intense meditation on the Lord's Person – examining the unspeakable gift, even Him 'in whom dwells all the fulness of the Godhead bodily.' Never are we ourselves in a better frame for departing than when enabled by the spirit of wisdom and revelation to gaze on the Lord Jesus, and claim that Mercy–seat, and that Ark with all its contents, as our own. Never do we realise so well what it is to be separate from earth and enter the suburbs of heaven as when thus engrossed with Him who is our Plant of Renown, with all its fruit and foliage, freshness and fragrance, beauty and shade. Sitting, in such an hour, at the feet of Him who has 'the keys of death and the invisible world,' we are almost already ushered over the threshold.

2. But our attention is fixed more directly still upon the Person of the Lord Jesus, when we turn to the blessed hope, His Second Coming. The glories of that day are such, in themselves and in their influence on us, as to guide our eye to Him personally, and keep it resting on Him. When a believer is enabled to meditate much and often on 'that blessed hope, and the glorious appearing of Him who is the Great God and our Saviour, Jesus Christ,' his soul catches from afar something of the glory yet to be revealed – not unlike to what poetry has sung of the cheerful bird, 'the messenger of day,' which in the early dawn pours out its melody, soaring all the while higher and higher

> – until the unrisen sun
> Gleams on its breast.

The believer, rapt into the future in his earnest anticipations, catches beams of that Better Sun which is yet to rise with healing on his wings. If the redeemed may say at death, 'As for me, I will behold thy face in righteousness' (Ps. 17:15), much more may they add, in hope of that resurrection day, 'I shall be satisfied when I wake with His likeness,' as if the rays of that morning were already shining on them with transforming power.

It shall be the Lamb Himself that shall lead each believer up from his quiet grave – ' The dead shall hear the voice of the Son of God' (John 5:25). As in the hour of conversion, awakening from their wordly dreams, they saw that stupendous sight, the Son of Man lifted up on the cross (John 3:3-14), so in the hour of the First Resurrection, they shall see His face again, not now marred, but become the seat of majesty, glory, beauty, as well as holy love. The Lamb Himself shall then lead them to living fountains and feed them as a shepherd (Rev. 7:17); and this will keep the thoughts of the glorified for ever on Himself. He is still their sun, whence beam forth light, and life, and joy – light, life, joy, worthy of the sore travail of His soul, worthy of His strong cries, worthy of His endless merits.

Why is it that we hope for That Day? Let John reply, 'When he shall appear, we shall be like him; for we shall see him as he is' (1 John 3:2). Or let Paul tell how he, and Clement, and Epaphroditus, and the saints of Caesar's household, and all the believers whom he knew, anticipated that day. He says that it was the Lord Himself they delighted to look for. It was not so much the triumphs of that day, nor its palms, and crowns, and white robes, and shouts of Hallelujah over sorrows for ever vanished; but it was the thought of the Lord Himself being there that made that day so joyful. 'Our conversation is in heaven, whence also we look for the Saviour, the Lord Jesus Christ' (Phil. 3:20). And when they associated their own blessedness with these anticipations, it was in this form – 'We shall be LIKE HIM.' 'He shall change our vile body that it may be fashioned LIKE UNTO HIS GLORIOUS BODY!'

What is this that Isaiah promises? 'The Lord shall be unto her an everlasting light, and thy God thy glory!' (Isa. 60:19). No stretch of thought can conceive the amount of honour and bliss expressed in these few words. And what is this that the same prophet promises to each one that now walks with God? He says, happy soul, 'Thine eyes shall see the king in his beauty' (Isa. 33:17). This is the highest hope He can hold out to thee; this is the greatest of His rewards; this is His best joy. Thine eyes shall see, and not be dim ; thine eyes shall see, and not be dazzled into blindness; thine eyes shall see, and gaze with calm and constant delight on 'the King in His beauty'. This is a promise of a true Transfiguration–day to thee. What was it that led the astonished multitude at the foot of the hill to run to the Son of Man as He descended from the scene of His brief Transfiguration? (Mark. 9:15). What caused that assembly to salute Him with such reverence? Was it not the impression produced on them by even a few lingering beams of glory, that hung on His form as the brightness did on Moses after his forty days' interview with God? And if that were so then, while He was seen under the returning clouds of sorrow, and while they who saw had not been fully anointed with the eye–salve that they might discern His real beauty, what may we not expect to enjoy on that day when the prophet's words are realised, 'Thine eyes shall see the King in His beauty!'

Are you a disciple whose eyes are often wistfully turned to the heavens, like the men of Galilee on the day of His ascension? You shall not always gaze in vain: 'Thine eyes shall see the King in His beauty.' Thou shalt see Him who is 'The fellow of the Almighty,' and yet also 'man' (Zech. 13:7); who can tell of 'men being His fellows' at the very moment that the Father proclaims Him 'God' (Heb. 1:9); whose human countenance, lighted up now with the 'joy unspeakable and full of glory,' tells what ecstasy is found in the Father's love; who is the brightness of the Father's glory, the express image of His person, revealing Godhead to the very sense of the creature, in a manner so attractive and heart–satisfying that the song of rapturous delight never has a pause.

Art thou a weary pilgrim? Walk on a little longer with thine eye still toward the Right Hand of the Majesty on high; for soon thou shalt see 'the King in His beauty.' Hast thou been vexed, like righteous Lot, from day to day, in seeing and learning earth's wickedness? Hast thou been saddened by witnessing death ravaging families, and removing some of thine own dearest ones? Hast thou but dimly descried amid thy tears the form of Him who walked on the sea at midnight to reassure His dejected and trembling disciples? Hast thou often been disappointed when thou didst think thou hadst got a look of things within the veil that would for ever turn thine eyes from beholding vanity? – Be of good cheer, 'Thine eyes shall see the King in His beauty.' Thy heaven shall consist in seeing Him as He is – knowing Him as He knoweth thee.

Among all the rewards offered to those who overcome, by the Captain of Salvation (when, after a sixty years' absence, He visited His suffering disciple in Patmos face to face), none is so magnificent, none so soul–filling, as that wherein He offers Himself in His glory. In this promised reward He may be said to offer us to Himself at the time when all His own reward has been bestowed, and when Himself has been anointed with the oil of gladness above His fellows. He writes, 'To him that overcometh and keepeth My works unto the end, to him will I give power over the nations; and he shall rule them with a rod of iron; as the vessels of a potter shall they be broken to shivers, even as I received of My Father.' Is not this enough? No, not yet; one thing more and better still by far, 'And I will give him the Morning Star' (Rev. 2:28). That is, I will give him Myself at the time I appear as 'Bright and Morning Star' (Rev. 22:16), rising in our sky after a night of gloom, the harbinger of an endless day. The great bliss of that day is this, the gift of Christ Himself at a time when joy, peace, love, and glory, and the holiness, wisdom, power, and majesty of Godhead, are the beams that radiate from His person, and bathe those on whom He shines.

If, believer, you love much that Person of whom we have all along in these pages been speaking, then press on to the day of His coming, for then it is you are to get Him in His fullest glory. Then it is you are to get as your Redemption Him who has been your Wisdom, your

Righteousness, your Sanctification. That 'Tower of David' was long ago gifted to you, with all its armoury; but your time for entering on the possession of it is now when it is furnished with whatever is magnificent, and royal, and heavenly, and divine; creation's riches being stored up therein. You shall see the Lord Jesus as yours at a time when His own and the Father's glory, and the glory of His angels, all combine to set forth His person. 'And your look that day shall be (says one) that of an owner, not the shy gaze of a passer-by.' That Christ, on yonder throne, is mine! With all His glory He is mine! That King of Kings, that Lord of Lords in His royal apparel, is mine! That beloved Son, whom the Father delighteth to honour for evermore, is mine! All that He is, all that He has, is mine!

Does not this prospect make a present life seem dull? It pours contempt on earth's fairest scenes! It mocks ambition. It makes coveteousness appear folly and infatuation. It renders trial light and duty easy! Christ Himself ours! Ours on that day when 'His peace' and 'His joy' are at their height! Our life is discovered to be 'Christ' (Col. 3:4). Oh, what a Christ that day reveals! The more intently we pore over what is to arrive on that day, we do the more intently gaze on the Person of the Son of God. We are kept in the very posture in which the Gospel of His First Coming placed us. On the one hand, we find that His coming to die and overcome death sends us forward to the coming again of Him who so overcame; but on the other, no sooner are we in His presence, amid His own and the Father's glory, than, in grateful remembrance, we go back to Him as He appeared to us in His low estate – these two views of Him so act and react on each other, combining to keep us ever in the attitude of beholding Himself.

There is to be no new Gospel for ever; and can there be need of any? The coming of the Lord shall fully unveil His Person, in whom all the Gospel is stored up. The feast of fat things full of marrow, in Isaiah 25:6, is the visible, as well as inward, discovery of His matchless person, in the day of His glory, when the pure canopy of the New Heavens, and the beauty shed over a Restored Creation, with all the teeming luxuriance of its hills and plains, and the melody of attendant harpers harping on the harps of heaven, shall be all but forgotten because of the presence of the 'King in His beauty.' Called in from the hedges and highways (Matt. 22:1-10), we feast even at present on fragments of this greater feast; but we get as yet little more than the crumbs – for little indeed do we see of the real glory of the Lord.

The Holy Spirit then, even as now, will continue to glorify Christ. There will be a fully unveiled Christ before us, and also there will be in us the Holy Spirit (unresisted by us and no longer grieved), springing up to eternal life, showing us His beauty. One difference only will there be – at present He gives us but drops, then He will pour upon us the horn of oil; and so shall we enter into the full joy of the Lord, not a scale left on our eye, nor one film left of the earthly mist that used to prevent our seeing Him who is the Image of God. The days of eternity shall pass on, and our eye shall never weary of looking on Him, but 'shall gaze upon His glories, as the eagle is said to do upon the meridian sun.' Ages upon ages pass, and still He is to us all in all. We admit the light from His Person freely now; never did Moses so eagerly survey the goodly land from Pisgah, as we now survey the glories of the Lamb. We get looks into that heart where love has dwelt from everlasting, and where love shall dwell to everlasting. Eternity is in its full course! Long, long ago, we lost sight of the shores of time, and still He is the unexhausted and inexhaustible fountain to us of 'Good tidings of Great Joy!' Eternity only serves to let in upon our souls the fulness of the blessing given to us in the day when we received Him, and began to have fellowship in His Gospel. The Gospel is still 'THE EVERLASTING GOSPEL'; for Christ is its substance; Christ is its essence; Christ is its Alpha and Omega; and the life it has brought us is out of 'Christ our life,' and must be 'Life Everlasting.'

Henceforth, then, this one thing I do: 'I count all things but loss for the excellency of the knowledge of Jesus Christ our Lord. I do count them but dung that I may win Christ, and that I may know Him. I follow after if that I may apprehend that for which also I am apprehended of Christ Jesus. I forget those things which are behind, and reach forth unto those things which are before – I press toward the mark for the prize of the high calling of God, in Christ Jesus' (Phil. iii. 8-10, 12, 14). Dr Owen spent some of the best years of his life in writing the *Treatise on the Person of Christ,* and some of his last days in preparing for the press his *Meditations on the Glory of Christ.* On the very day he died, a friend came to tell him that his book was now in the press, at which he expressed satisfaction. 'But, O Brother,' said he, 'the long looked for day is come at last, in which I will see that glory in another manner than I have ever done yet, or was capable of doing in this world!'

O Holy Spirit, grant that all of us may be found by the Lord when He calls, or when He comes, thus occupied in meditation on His Person and Glory, ready to start up at the call, saying to one another, 'O Brother, the looked for day is come at last!'

Appendix

EXTRACTS FROM OLD AUTHORS

'God would have us pitch our faith upon The Person of His Son, and not barely upon the Promise. And therefore, He has so ordered things in His divine wisdom that the Promises should all hold on Christ, and be Yea and Amen in Him.' – (TILLINGHAST's Six Sermons, p. 9).

'Saving faith is in the nature of it not a mere assent to a testimony, but a receiving and resting upon The Person of Jesus Christ alone, for salvation both from sin and wrath, and unto all the grace and glory of God.' – (CUDWORTH's Experience, p. 10).

'Those Divines who in their Catechetical Systems have made the formal object of Faith to be the Promise, rather than The Person of Christ, have failed in their expressions, if not in their intentions.' – (SPURSTOW on Rom. 6:1).

'Folk must go first to Christ's Person before they can get good of His offices. Folk must make a direct address to the Person of the Mediator before they reap His purchase. Pardon is sweet, adoption is sweet, grace is sweet, heaven is sweet; but Christ is sweeter. ' – (WEBSTER'S Sermons, p. 88).

'Faith does not marry the soul to the portion, benefits, and privileges of Christ, but to Christ Himself. I don't say that the soul may not have an eye to these, and a respect to these in closing with Christ; yea, usually these are the first things that faith has in its eye. But the soul does, and must go higher; he must look at and pitch upon The Person of Christ, or his faith is not so right and complete as it ought to be. It is The Person of Christ that is the great fountain of all grace and of all manifestations of God to us; and faith accordingly does close with His Person.' – (PEARSE's Best Match, p. 160).

Such delight had Samuel Rutherford in The Person of Christ that he writes to his friends such things as the following : – 'Holiness is not Christ; the blossoms and flavours of the Tree of Life are not the Tree itself' (Lett. 335). 'He, He Himself, is more excellent than heaven. Oh, what a life were it to sit beside this Well of Love, and drink and sing, sing and drink!' (Lett. 288). 'My greatest pain is want of Him; not of His joys and comforts, but of a near union and communion.' 'I have casten this work upon Christ, to get in Himself' (Lett. 187; Lett. 112). 'I would be farther in upon Christ than at His joys, in where love and mercy lodgeth – beside His heart !' (Lett. 286). 'Oh, if I could doat as much upon Himself as I do upon His love!' (Lett. 160). 'I would fain learn not to idolise comfort, sense, joy, and sweet–felt presence. All these are but creatures, and nothing but the kingly robe, the golden ring, the bracelets of the Bridegroom. The Bridegroom Himself is better than all ornaments that are about Him' (Lett. 168). 'If the comparison could stand, I would not exchange Christ with heaven itself' (Lett. 111).

Once more. A century ago, Romaine (Life of Faith, p. 159) thus wrote in expounding the verses 1 John 2:13-14, – ' Many continue little children and weak in faith, because they do not presently attain a solid acquaintance with The Person of Christ.'

The sum of the matter is this. There is a vast difference between, on the one hand, believing day by day in a living Saviour, and on the other, resting satisfied with the salvation He brings, as if that were all.

Also available from Christian Focus Publications...

ANDREW BONAR AND R.M. MCCHEYNE

MISSION OF DISCOVERY

THE BEGINNINGS OF MODERN JEWISH EVANGELISM

The journal of Bonar and McCheyne's Mission of Inquiry

ISBN 978–1–85792–258–5

Mission of Discovery

The Beginnings of Modern Jewish Evangelism

R.M. McCheyne and Andrew Bonar

The journal of Bonar and McCheyne's Mission of inquiry, 1839. This epic chronicle has a fascination that stems from the attention to detail both men had for what they saw. It is part travel book, adventure story, and social history. This is an absorbing story of the scattered Jewish people of the mid-nineteenth century and the problems of travel in politically unstable situations. As a result of this journey, the first Church of Scotland missionary to the Jews was sent to Hungary in 1841.

Christian Focus Publications

Our mission statement –

STAYING FAITHFUL

In dependence upon God we seek to impact the world through literature faithful to His infallible Word, the Bible. Our aim is to ensure that the Lord Jesus Christ is presented as the only hope to obtain forgiveness of sin, live a useful life and look forward to heaven with Him.

Our books are published in four imprints:

CHRISTIAN FOCUS

Popular works including bio-graphies, commentaries, basic doctrine and Christian living.

CHRISTIAN HERITAGE

Books representing some of the best material from the rich heri-tage of the church.

MENTOR

Books written at a level suitable for Bible College and seminary students, pastors, and other seri-ous readers. The imprint includes commentaries, doctrinal studies, examination of current issues and church history.

CF4•K

Children's books for quality Bible teaching and for all age groups: Sunday school curriculum, puzzle and activity books; personal and fam-ily devotional titles, biographies and inspirational stories – because you are never too young to know Jesus!

Christian Focus Publications Ltd,
Geanies House, Fearn, Ross–shire,
IV20 1TW, Scotland, United Kingdom.
www.christianfocus.com